Millais

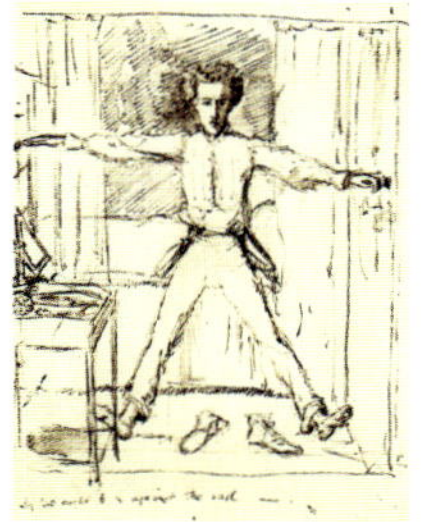

a Sketch

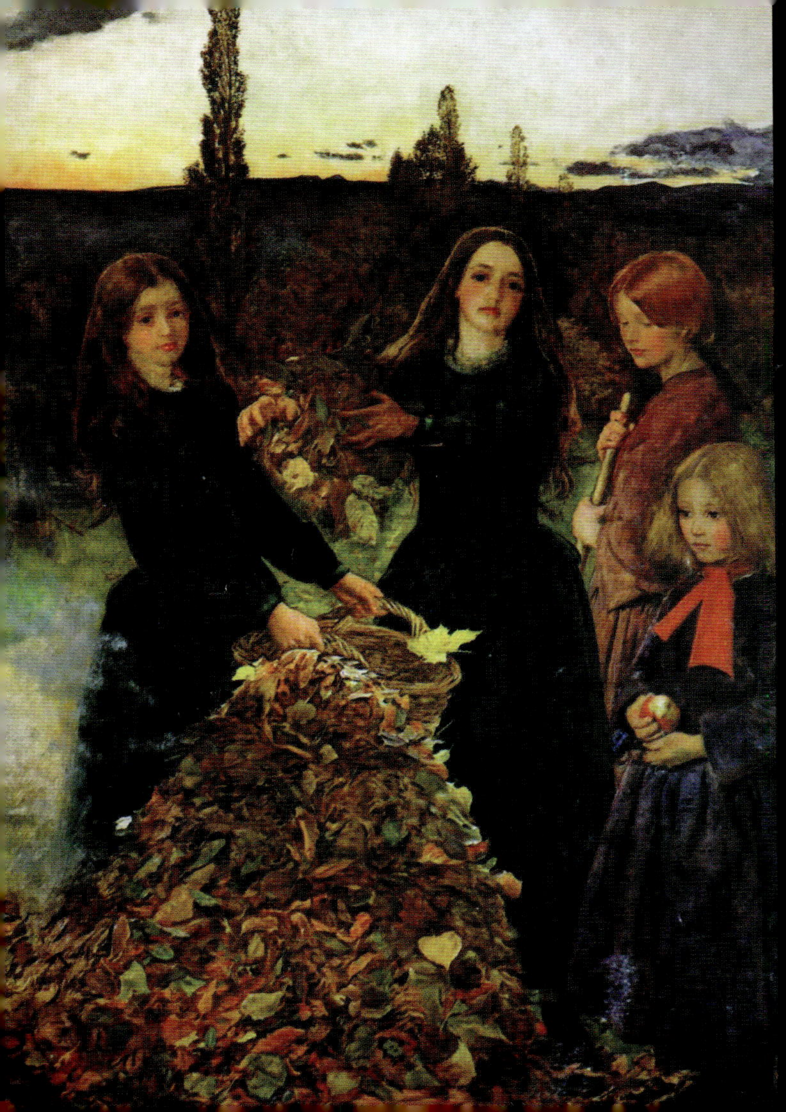

MILLAIS

A SKETCH

BY

MARION HARRY SPIELMANN

PRECEDED BY

THOUGHTS ON OUR ART OF TODAY

BY

JOHN EVERETT MILLAIS

with an introduction by

JASON ROSENFELD

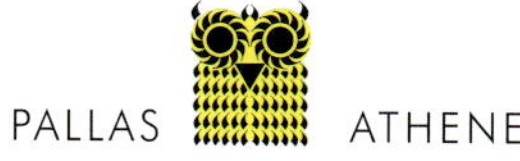

PALLAS ATHENE

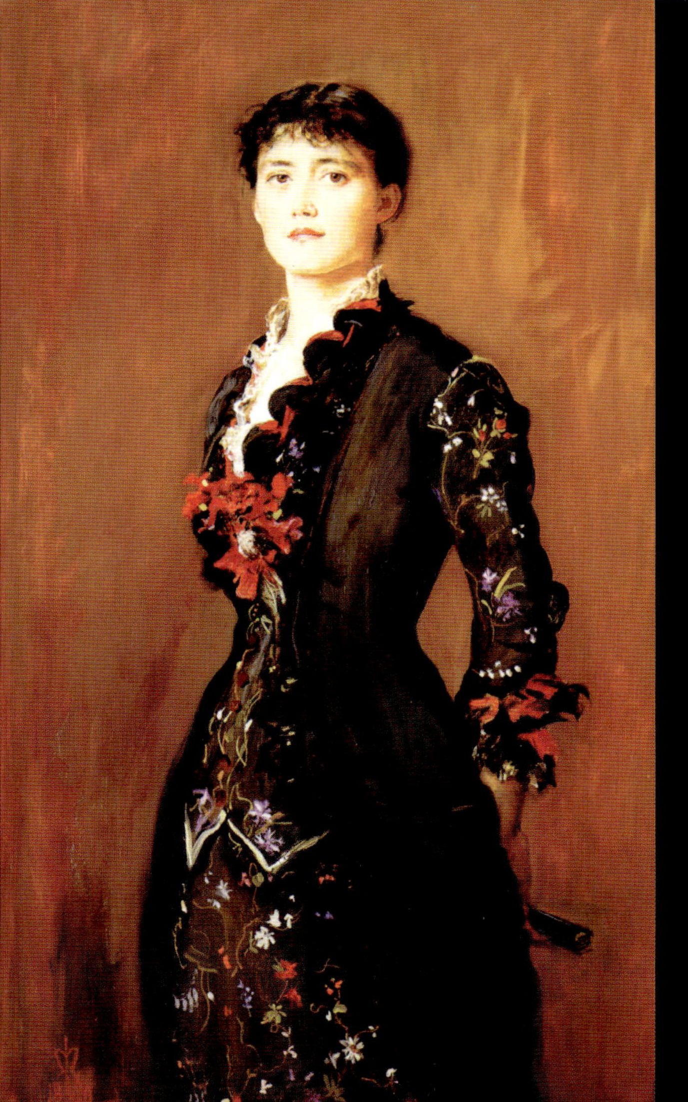

CONTENTS

Opposite title page: Autumn Leaves, 1855-6
Opposite: Louise Jopling, 1879

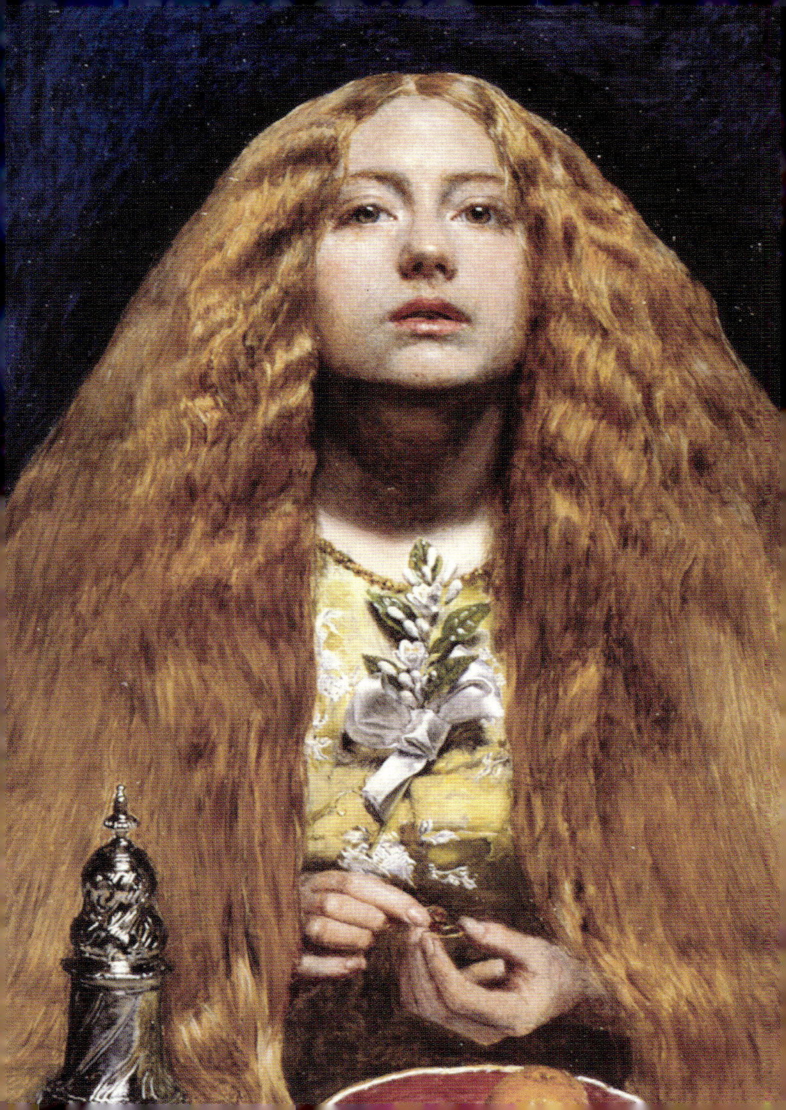

INTRODUCTION

JASON ROSENFELD

Millais was just eleven when he entered the Royal Academy of Arts (RA) schools, still to this day their youngest ever student. All signs pointed to the child prodigy following the standard career path of a Joshua Reynolds or a Thomas Lawrence. But in the autumn of 1848, Millais and six other art students including Dante Gabriel Rossetti and William Holman Hunt formed the secret Pre-Raphaelite Brotherhood (PRB), in a challenge to contemporary aesthetics that Rossetti would later describe as 'the visionary vanities of half-a-dozen boys'. He was half correct. For Pre-Raphaelitism was indeed visionary, as well as radical, transforming every genre its artists worked in, from portraiture to landscape to religious and historical paintings. And Millais was its most talented practitioner. While the PRB channelled art from before the time of the followers of Raphael in order to invigorate the art of the present, the Brothers did not

Opposite: The Bridesmaid, 1851

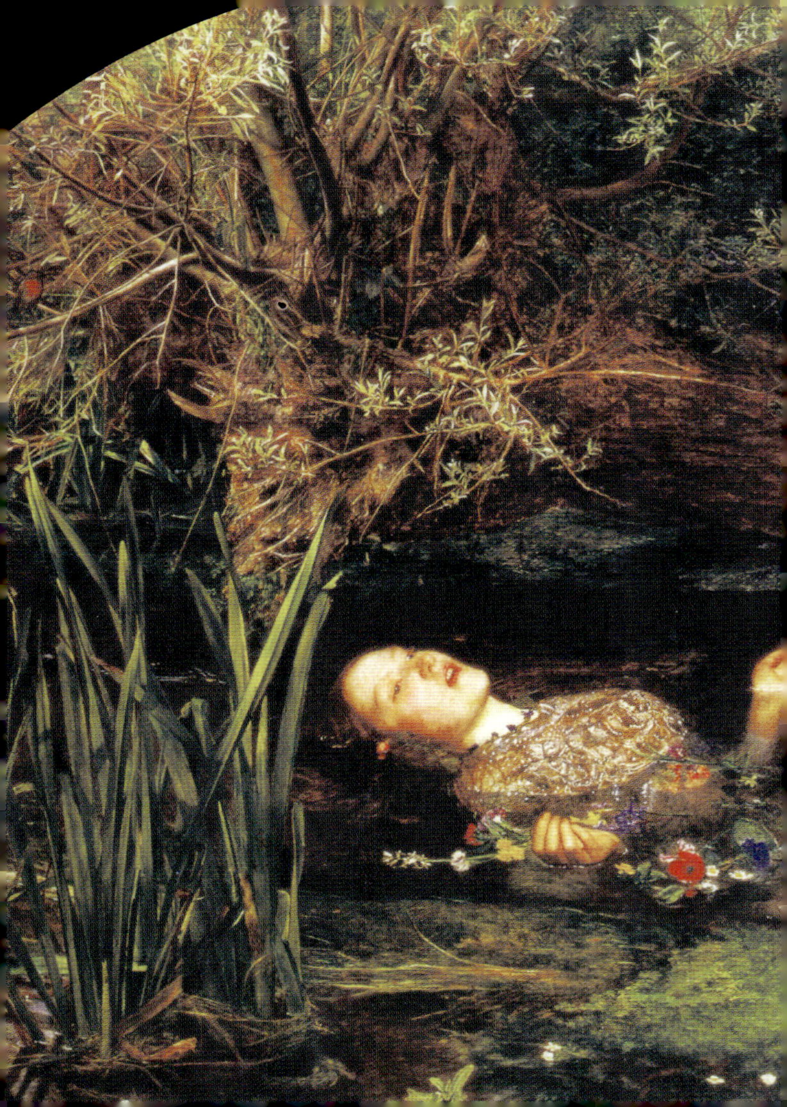

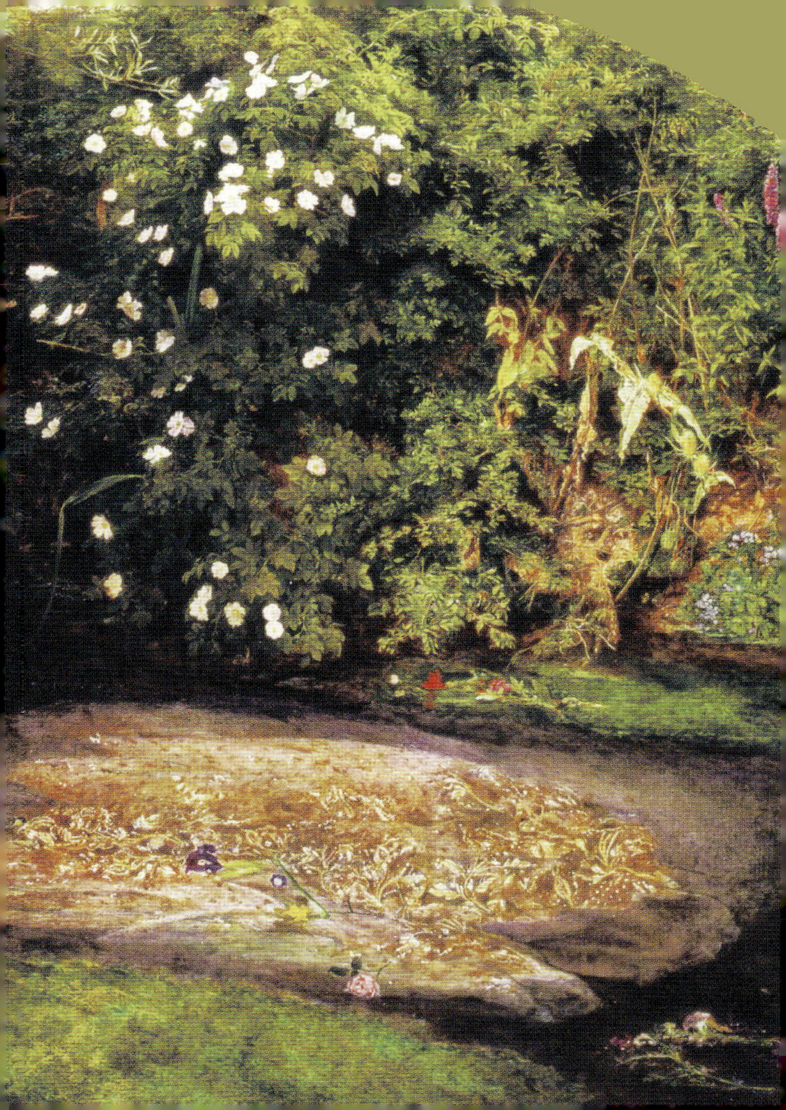

simply look back to early Italian painting, or Netherlandish works, but instead used the most modern materials and depended on their own perceptive abilities to rethink both the process and product of art in the 1840's and 50's. Hunt may have been the most committed member of the movement in terms of theory and religiosity, and Rossetti its most poetic and literarily romantic, but Millais was its most creative member, and his pictures the most varied. The sheer quality and distinctness of each of his paintings of the 1850's is unmatched by any Western artist of the period.

But Millais was no natural rebel. He never forswore the RA, where he was protected by a number of academicians amenable to his aims and awed by his talent; and indeed it can be tempting to see his subsequent career as a yielding to academicism, and the Victorian appetite for jingo, mawkishness and sentiment. Certainly there is no gainsaying his public success, which earned him a substantial fortune, the life of a gentleman (including considerable time spent fishing, shooting and stalking), a baronetcy and something approaching a state funeral. And he

Previous pages: Ophelia, 1851-52

Opposite: The Woodman's Daughter, 1851-52

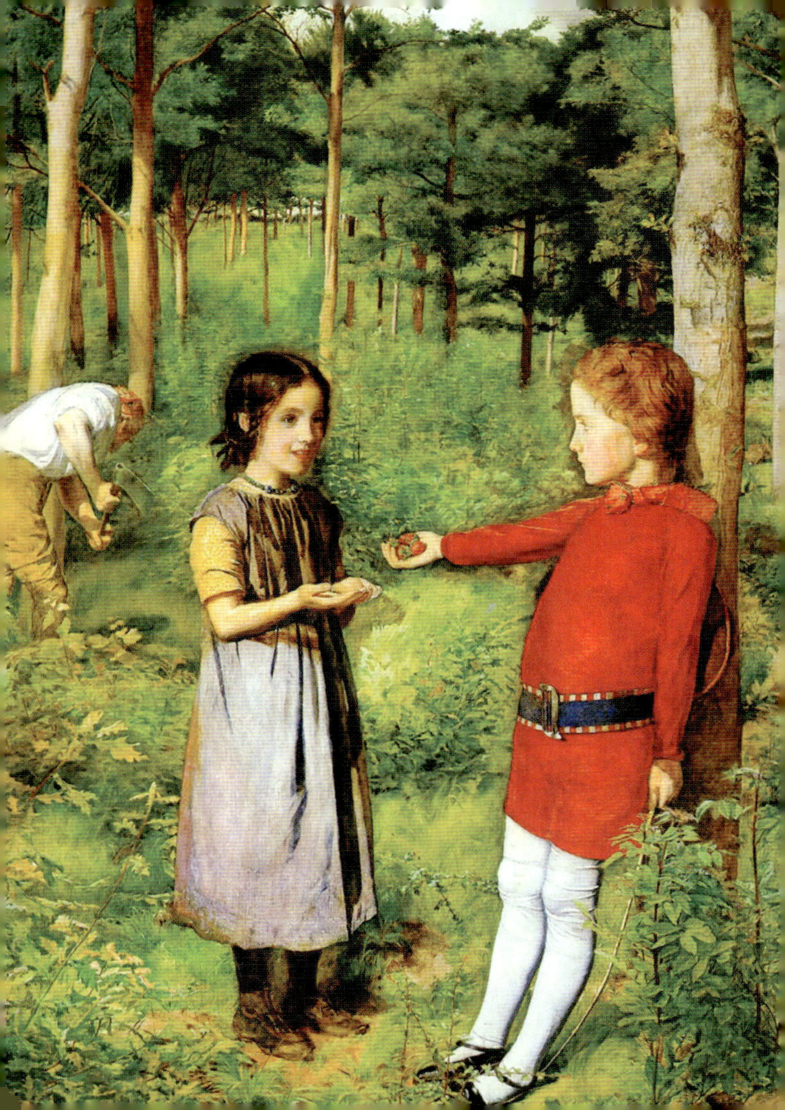

certainly could paint with an eye to the imperial theme with history paintings such as The North-West Passage *(Tate) and* The Boyhood of Raleigh *(Tate). In time he came to be acknowledged as the nation's portraitist, with canonical images of eminent leaders and artists such as Gladstone (NPG, Christ Church, Oxford), Disraeli (NPG), Tennyson (Lady Lever Art Gallery), Bulwer-Lytton (V&A), – paintings against which small scale black-and-white photographs, despite that medium's claim to authenticity of likeness, did not stand a chance.*

Yet it would be a mistake to see Millais' post-Brotherhood career simply as a sell-out. Rather, his abandonment of the tightly painted and hallucinatorily bright Pre-Raphaelite style, with its heavy dependence on literary sources, was a move towards a looser, less strident style more apt to appeal to the sense and to the viewer's personal experience. This is evident in his most resonant work, Autumn Leaves *(1855-6; Manchester City Art Gallery), with its novel construction of female beauty (castigated at the time as vulgar) and nostalgic tone. Such works presage the Aesthetic Movement in British art and its call for a subjectless 'art for art's sake'. At the same time, Millais honed his delicacy of touch and*

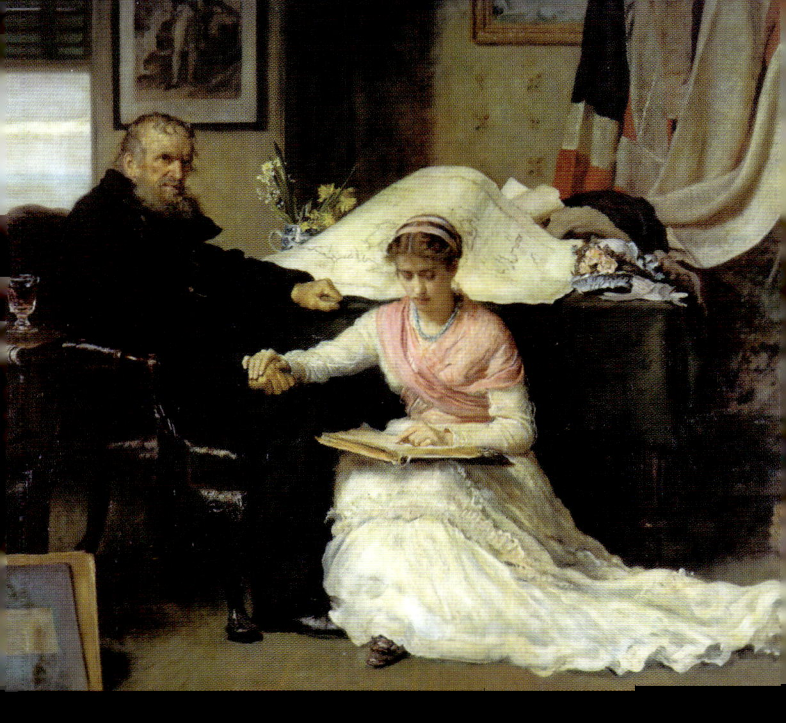

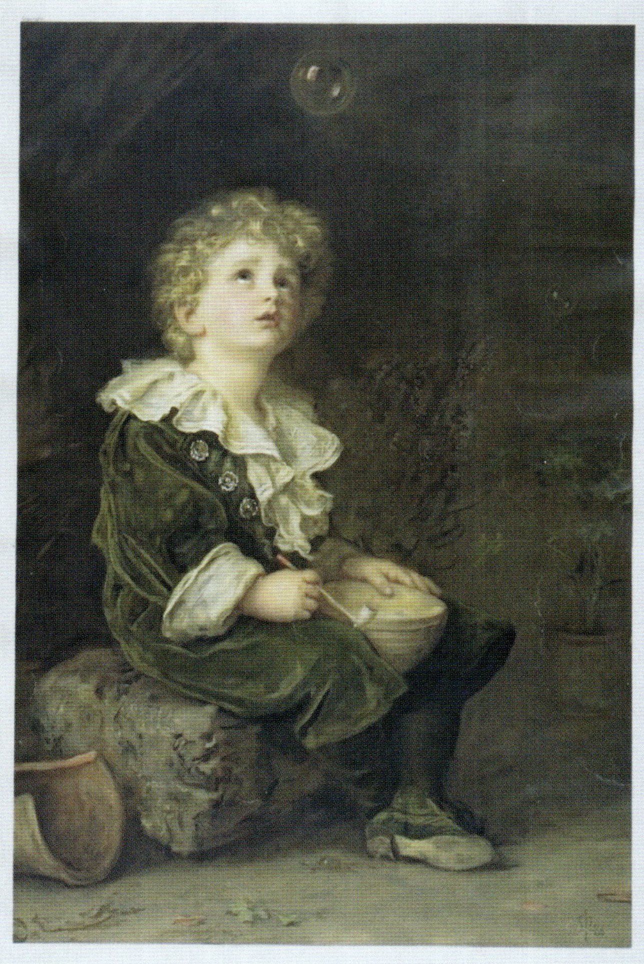

BUBBLES.

From the Original Painting by the late Sir John E. Millais B.t President of the Royal Academy
in the possession of Messrs Pears.

psychological acuity in his book and periodical illustrations, producing masterly and topical work for authors such as Trollope, Tennyson and Collins.

If we keep this innovative, affective approach in mind, it will not only allow us to appreciate more fully the psychological interest of paintings like The Boyhood of Raleigh, *but also to appreciate more sympathetically the 'fancy pictures' whose reputation has perhaps sunk lowest of all Millais' work. These portraits, often of children, reprised 18th century examples by Reynolds, Romney and Gainsborough and were eagerly consumed in the form of prints in popular journals after works like* Cherry Ripe *(private collection) and in their use in advertising as in the famous case of* Bubbles *(Unilever, on loan to Lady Lever Art Gallery). These pictures, while not his most important works (and the artist himself never claimed they were), nonetheless represent a continuity of humanism in Millais, portraying children not solely as doll-like bearers of romantic ideals of innocence but, rather, as conveyors of a deep sense of inner life.*

It is this essential humanity – so unexpected after the Pre-Raphaelite work – that is the leit-motif of M. H.

Opposite: Bubbles, 1886, in a chromolithograph of the following year

Spielmann's valedictory Sketch of Millais' *life, reprinted in this volume. Spielmann (1858-1948) was a highly successful journalist and editor of* The Magazine of Art. *This staid publication Spielmann transformed after his arrival in 1887 into a cheerleader for British art. For perhaps the first time, artists were treated as celebrities and personalities, their names printed in capital letters to jump out at the reader. Exhibitions were trailed, works promoted, networks of contacts established. Spielmann was particularly tireless in soliciting artists to write criticism and give readers insights into their thinking and practice.*

The magazine's former antipathy to Millais' work of the 1860's was quickly reversed, and within a year of Spielmann's arrival Millais was persuaded to contribute his Thoughts on the art of today, *reprinted here. These remain the artist's only published reflections on painting. The essay is pithy rather than scintillating – Millais was better with paint than in print, and he knew it – but is heartfelt and illuminating. Some of the essay addresses painterly issues such as the disastrous use of asphaltum by Reynolds and others in the cause of pleasing conventional taste (the excellent condition of Millais' own paintings show how careful he was as a technician). But the main theme of the essay is Millais' call for individuality and variety in art, a trait evident in his own exceptional powers of invention across his entire career. His concluding preference for Rembrandt's ability to conceal the 'whole science of painting' in his late works, over Velázquez' too evident power of execution may come as a surprise. For the Old Master artist Millais was most linked to in his lifetime was the Spaniard, but Millais' late works, the landscapes in particular, bear closer links with this idea of Rembrandt and the spirit of the Ovidian tag* Ars celare artem: *it is art to conceal art. For Millais, true art emerges from labour and experience, the workings of which are invisible to the uninitiated but which hold the key, as Ruskin had written of Turner decades before, to aesthetic revelation.*

These late landscapes are the object of some of Spielmann's greatest enthusiasm. Almost forgotten today, this remarkable series of over twenty large-scale landscapes was painted in the out-of-doors in Perthshire over Millais' long summer holidays. These are a revelation – each individualistic, none picturesque nor Impressionistic, a poetic compilation of Turner and Constable sharpened by Millais' own exacting eye.

Overleaf: Chill October, 1870

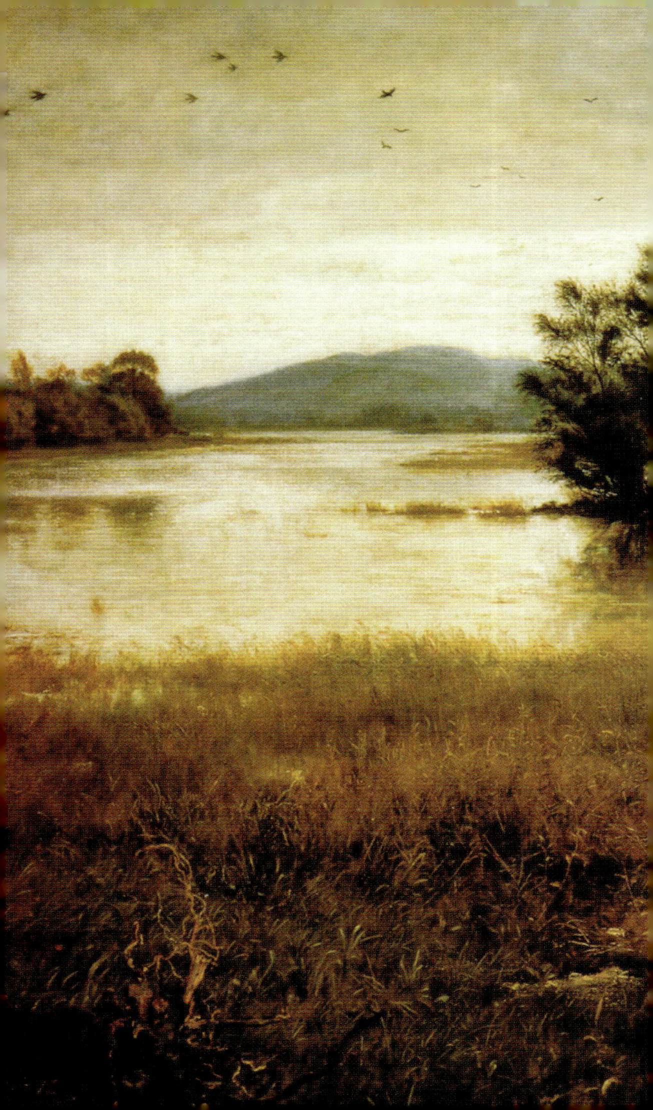

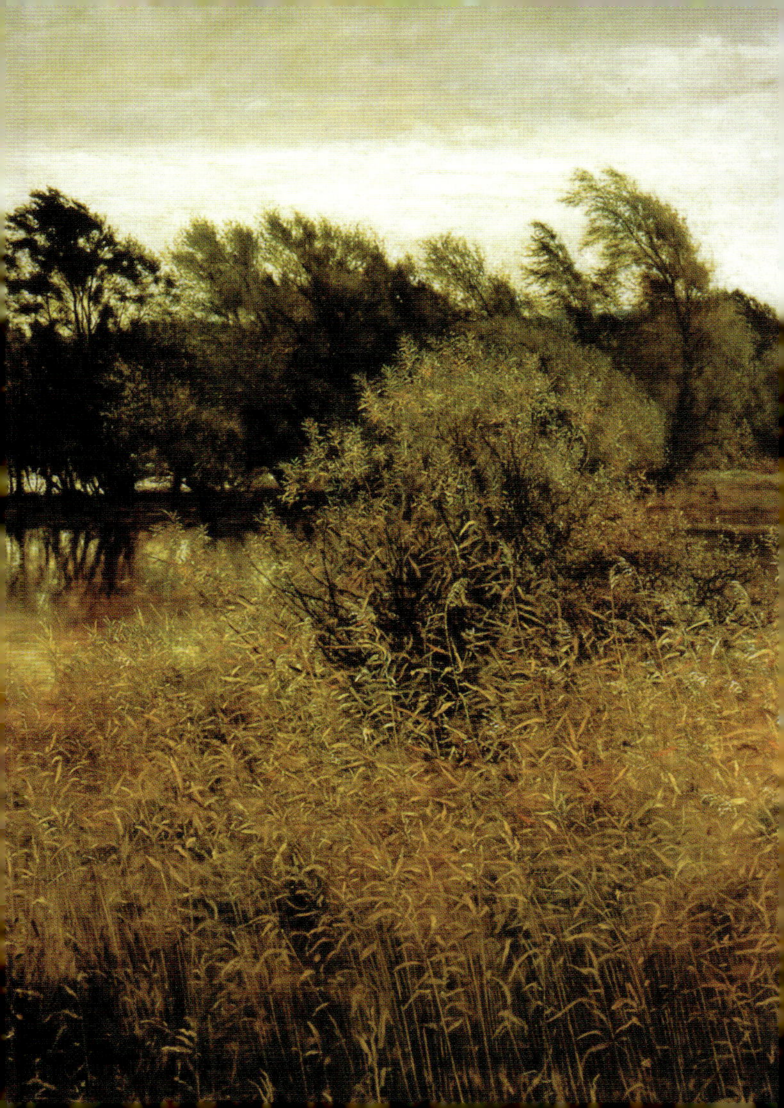

Millais' article was successful enough to provoke a rejoinder from Watts, who called it 'crisp and interesting' and then took issue on the subject of Old Master technique. Spielmann meanwhile remained close to Millais for the remaining eight years of the artist's life, up to the last miserable months when Millais, the cheerful and fluent talker, was struck dumb by cancer of the throat – an agony with which Spielmann unexpectedly opens the Sketch. *Although this intimate and suitably Victorian introduction testifies to the very personal affection in which Millais was held by both Spielmann and Spielmann's public, the* Sketch *in fact focusses clearly on Millais' work; his personality and private life are only touched on in the context of the work. There is little about Millais the social or the family man with eight children, though his runaway marriage with Effie Ruskin was one of the most astonishing love scandals of the Victorian era, and it was Millais' last request of Queen Victoria that she receive Effie, hitherto not acceptable at court. (The Queen graciously complied.) Nor is there much attention paid to Millais' public spiritedness in facilitating the foundation of the National Portrait Gallery, the Tate, or the Artists'*

Opposite: Waiting, 1854; the figure may be Effie

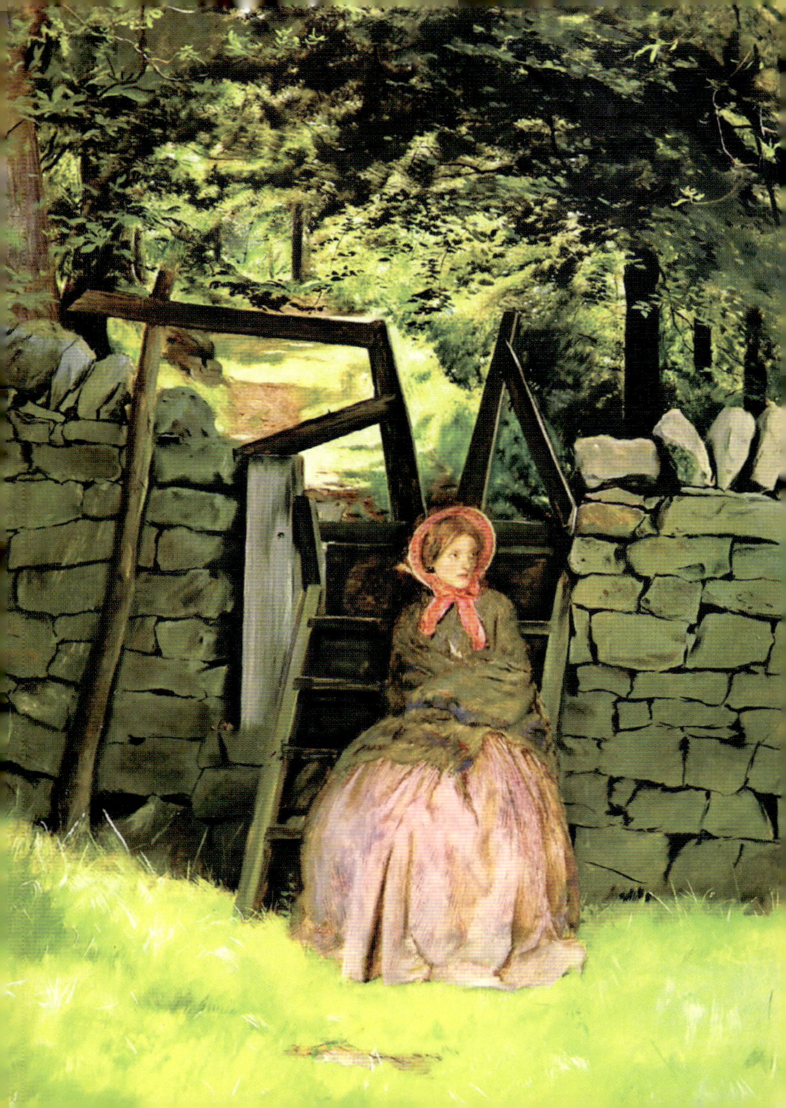

Benevolent Fund. Spielmann's focus on the work is partly a function of the Sketch's *place as an introduction to the guidebook he wrote to the RA memorial exhibition of Millais' paintings, but it is also recognition of the fact that this is the first concerted and measured assessment of Millais' career. For although Millais had been written about more frequently than almost any other artist of the era, there was little of an informed, first person or analytic nature, with the exception of occasional criticism by Millais's fellow Pre-Raphaelites, F. G. Stephens and W. M. Rossetti. Even Ruskin, for all his involvement with the Pre-Raphaelite Brotherhood, and with Millais personally, never wrote a concentrated piece on the artist.*

In starting with Millais' death, which he pairs with that of Leighton only seven months earlier, Spielmann also recognized that it represented a moment to reflect on the achievements of English art in the 19th century. Spielmann's memorial article on Leighton, whom Millais had replaced as president of the Royal Academy, in The Magazine of Art *is in striking contrast to his pæan to Millais. Leighton, the foreign-trained classicist, is described as an excellent promoter of the arts, administrator, the greatest president the RA ever had, and an intellectual. But Spielmann was critical of the 'corrupting influence of Florentine flesh-painting' on his art, and speckled his text with negative comments on his works and unflattering quotations from estimable commentators like Ford Madox Brown and John Ruskin. By contrast, Millais was the home-grown prodigy, the true and manly Englishman, the accessible painter whom the public clearly felt it knew more intimately than the private Leighton.*

Unsurprisingly, the Pre-Raphaelite episode is treated cautiously, Spielmann disassociating its members from bohemianism, and downgrading their radicalism to a degree, betraying his intolerance of 'agitation for agitation's sake' in subsequent movements. It is a somewhat reactionary portrait. But it was important for Spielmann nevertheless to establish Pre-Raphaelitism as the wellspring for modern British art. Millais is portrayed on the wider stage as representative of British nationalism in his art, and on a smaller stage as the quintessential English gentleman. Spielmann describes the soaring trajectory of Millais' career, seeing it with hindsight in the 1890s as an unstoppable flight (though there had been many periods of unpopularity in the early years), culminating in a reputation that must have seemed unassailable. Spielmann's conclusion reveals his personal investment in both Millais and the art of his time, as well as his grander sense of history. He subconsciously conveys the idea that talents close to us that we may have been privileged to know, to see at work, to be intimate with, are for all time and rise in importance. At the time of his death there was indeed little questioning of Millais' importance in the popular, international, or specialized press. Millais was a man towards whom few bore enmity, not even Ruskin, whose criticism of his works was often glowing, even after his wife had left him for the painter. Genuineness was Millais' chief characteristic. He carried the charming braggadocio of one who had earned success but, the generous temperament, evident from a young age, meant that he rarely riled his peers and associates. Spielmann's coda to his memorial appreciation may seem excessively flowery in sentiment, and indeed it is – unapologetically so. The heartfelt is a somewhat lost craft in journalism today. Millais inspired it in many people. And that genuineness was conveyed in his art, which did not proselytize or preach or even inspire but, rather, aimed to touch.

JOHN EVERETT MILLAIS

Thoughts on our art of today

from
The Magazine of Art
1888

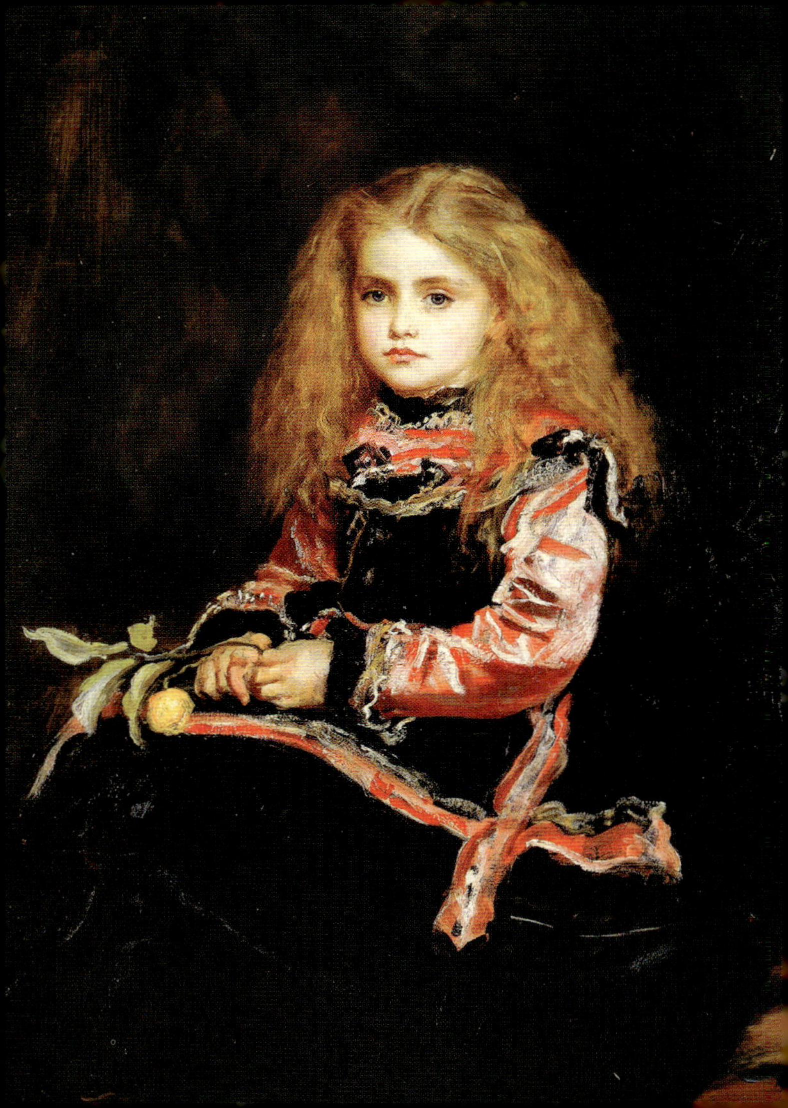

I am emphatically of opinion that the best Art of modern times is as good as any of its kind that has gone before, and furthermore, that the best Art of England can hold its own against the world. It is manifestly impossible to make just comparisons between the widely divergent styles of the Ancient and Modern Masters, or to attempt to strike a balance between, say, Rubens and Hogarth; but to say that the old alone is good betrays great lack of judgement, and is an ingratitude to the living. Ability and talent are more abundant than ever; but in forming an opinion of them the critic falls into two great errors – the first, in forgetting that the form and demands of Art have changed and expanded with the advance of time; and the second, in failing – unconsciously, of course – to judge of the great works of the past, with which he compares those of the present, in a fair and proper manner. He makes no allowances for the charm of mutilation or the fascination of decay.

The only way to judge of the treasures the Old Masters of whatever age have left us – whether in architecture, sculpture, or painting – with any hope of sound deduction, is to look at the work and ask oneself – 'What was that like when it was new?' The

Opposite: Souvenir of Velasquez, 1868

Elgin Marbles are allowed by common consent to be the perfection of art. But how much of our feeling of reverence is inspired by Time? Imagine the Parthenon as it must have looked with the frieze of the mighty Phidias fresh from the chisel. Could one behold it in all its pristine beauty and splendour we should see a white marble building, blinding in the dazzling brightness of a southern sun, the figures of the exquisite frieze in all probability painted – there is more than a suspicion of that – and the whole standing against the intense blue sky; and many of us, I venture to think, would cry at once, 'How excessively crude!'

No; Time and Varnish are two of the greatest Old Masters, and their merits and virtues are too often attributed by critics – I do not of course allude to our professional art-critics – to the painters of the pictures they have toned and mellowed. The great artists all painted in *bright* colours, such as it is the fashion nowadays for men to decry as crude and vulgar, never suspecting that what they applaud in those works is merely the result of what they condemn in their contemporaries. Take a case in point – the *Bacchus and Ariadne* in the National Gallery, with its splendid red robe and its rich brown grass. You may rest assured that the painter of that bright red robe never painted the grass brown. He saw the colour as it was, and painted it as it was – distinctly green; only it has faded with time to its present beautiful mellow colour. Yet many men, nowadays, will not have a picture with green in it; there are even buyers who when giving a commission to an artist will stipulate that the canvas shall contain none of it. But God Almighty has given us green, and you may depend upon it it's a fine colour.

There is, and has been for a century or so, this growing cry for 'subdued colour'; and what is the result? The case of Sir Joshua Reynolds is a sufficiently notorious example. It was his custom – well knowing what he did – to paint in clear and true colours. We have it from Walpole, after a visit to Reynolds' studio, that he found the Waldegrave picture, which now commands so much admiration for its mellowness of tone, 'dreadfully white and pinky.' But Sir George Beaumont, the connoisseurs, and patrons, were forever urging him to give them in his pictures what time alone can effect: 'tone – like the Old Masters.' And at length, to satisfy their reiterated demands, he made use of the pigment that would most readily give the rich soft brown they wanted –

Overleaf: Hearts are Trumps (Portraits of Elizabeth, Diana and Mary, Daughters of Walter Armstrong, Esq.), 1872

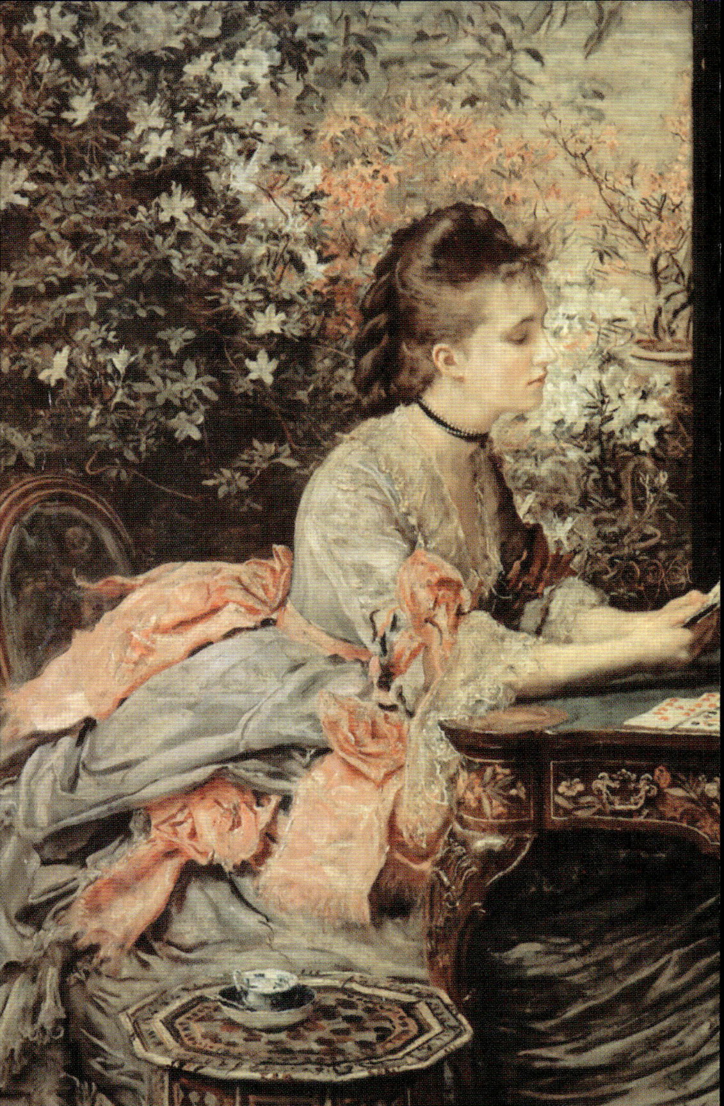

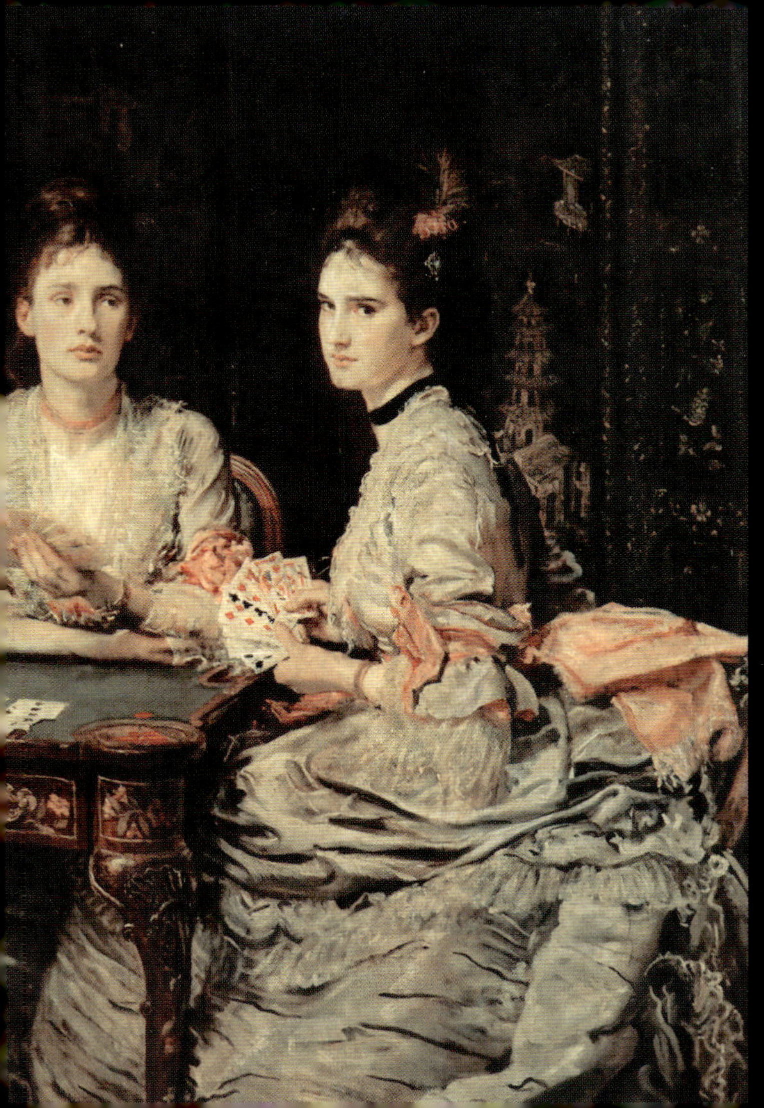

asphaltum. And now every picture that contains that villainous colour is in every stage of decomposition and ruin – and the chief responsibility for that lies heavily on his critics.

I began by expressing my faith in our English school of painting and its performance. A hundred years hence, when Time has done its work, that school will receive the approval of posterity. It must be remembered, however, that Art has moved with the age, not only in the matter of its subject and the spirit which pervades it, but also in knowledge and technical skill. The still-life painting of the Ancients is even now held up to us as a wonder. We are told of the grapes of Zeuxis, which the birds came to peck at, and of Parrhasius' curtain that deceived Zeuxis, and so on. But what of that? That is mere imitation, and I could place my hand on half a dozen men who could do as much. Not that I underrate imitative painting for a moment – it is a necessary part of an artist's business, and a high achievement in itself, this representing on the flat of the colour, texture, and chiaroscuro of a solid object in such a way as to deceive the eye. But it is hardly necessary to say that nowadays art demands much more than that.

I imagine that Greek painting was little more than *tinted outline*, no doubt so far as it went not less remarkable in its excellence than the sculpture of the day, but necessarily *primitive*, from their ignorance of the pigments since discovered. Only through the introduction of oil-painting has it been possible to arrive at the subtlety and mystery that are connected with fine workmanship – such execution as we enjoy in Rembrandt or in Titian, in Sir Joshua or in Turner. I will add that if you place a first-class Rembrandt, a first-class Reynolds, and, say, a first-class latter-day example, side by side, and judge them on the basis I have named – that is to say, making due allowances for the effects of time, and, of course, for the different styles and temperaments of the painters – you will find little cause to bewail the 'decadence of art.' On the contrary, there will be plenty of reason to be proud of your art of today, and to be confident for your art of the future.

But while we look around and congratulate our-selves on the number of young men whose brilliant talents hold out such bright promise of worthily upholding the English school, we must not forget that only by insistence upon their *individuality* of concep-tion and expression can they hope to advance to the first rank. There is among us a band of young men who, though English, persist in painting with a broken French accent, all of them much alike, and seemingly content to lose their identity in their imitation of French masters, whom they are constitutionally, absolutely, and in the nature of things unable to copy with justice either to themselves or to their models. Imitation, however, is pardonable in young men – *and only in young men* – and sooner or later their ability will inevitably lead them to assert their individuality if they have any. Any artist can be a follower without sacrificing one jot of his independence. Sir Edwin Landseer, for example, stands perfectly alone in his own sphere; yet as an animal-painter he was a follower of Snyder, but in no sense an imitator. Sir Frederick Leighton, again, though his grace, dignity, and beauty of flowing line are plainly inspired by the ideal Greek sculpture, works, if I may so express it, his own bicycle; everything he does is his and his alone. On the other hand, we see in the English sculpture of an era now, happily, just gone by, the result of what mere imitation had brought us to. Founded on the same type of Greek statue, Venuses, Dianas, the three Graces, and all the Virtues followed each other till they flooded the land, each as characterless as the last, and with no more individuality or vigour than if they had been turned out by machinery from a single mould. But the influence of Carpeaux, who was one of the leaders of the great French school of Sculpture and placed it above the rest of the modern world – strongly supported in the present day by M. Dalou – has at length reached us; and this department of art now augurs every whit as well for the future as that of painting.

So fine is some of the work our modern sculptors have given us, that I firmly believe that were it dug up from under oyster-shells in Rome or out of Athenian sands, with the *cachet* of partial dismemberment about it, all Europe would fall straightway into ecstasy and give forth their plaintive wail – 'We can do nothing like that now.' Verily the great handicapper and chief offending of modern art is its unavoidable modernity.

But individuality is not all that should be looked to; a varied manner must be cultivated as well. I believe that however admirably he may paint in a certain method, or however perfectly he may render a certain class of subject, the artist should not be content to adhere to a speciality of manner or method. A fine style is good, but it is not everything – it is not even absolutely necessary. Sir Joshua was much superior to Gainsborough in that regard; but who will give the palm between first-rate examples of these two masters? One loaded his canvas; the other painted as with water-colour. The incomparable

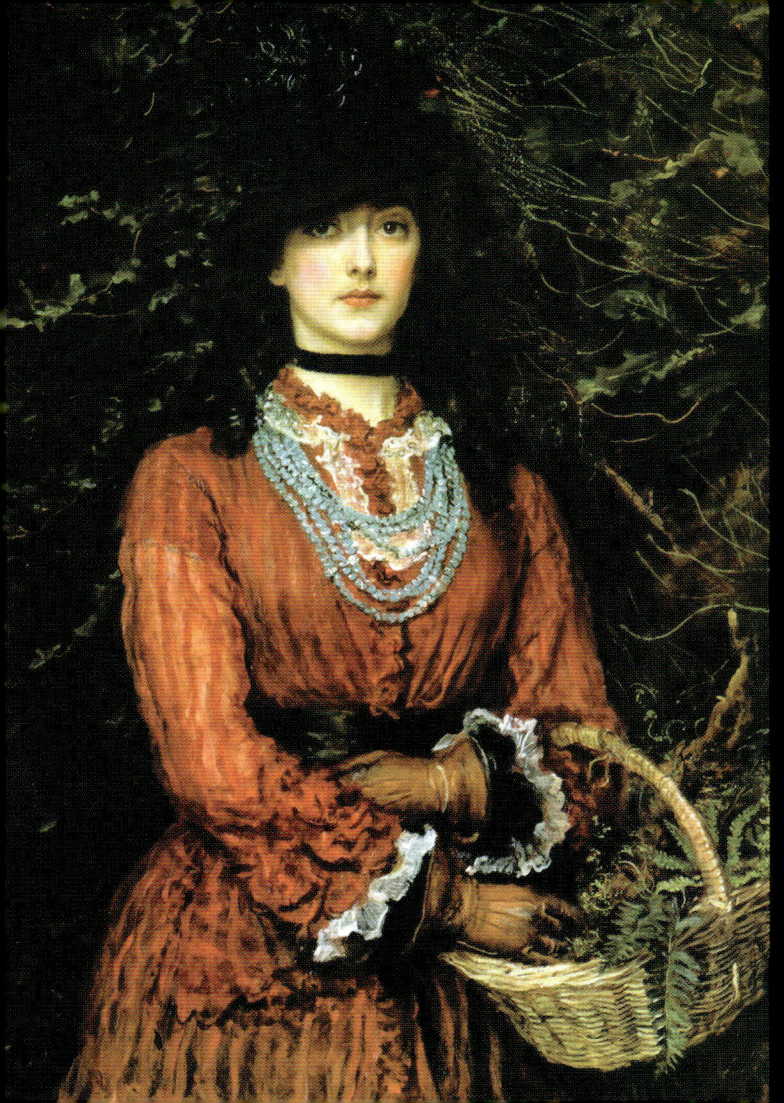

charm the latter imparted to his ladies makes one forget and forgive the want of body in his work, and we feel they are sufficiently delightful as they are. Of course, delicacy and energy, breadth or refinement of touch, may be varied with the mood and the character of the picture.

The commonest error into which a critic can fall is the remark we so often hear that such-and-such an artist's work is 'careless' and 'would be better had more labour been spent upon it.' As often as not this is wholly untrue. As soon as the spectator can *see* that more labour has been spent upon it he may be sure that the picture is to that extent incomplete and unfinished, while the look of freshness that is inseparable from a really successful picture would of necessity be absent. If the high finish of a picture is so apparent as immediately to force itself upon the spectator, he may *know* that it is not as it should be; and from the moment that the artist feels his work is becoming a labour he may depend upon it it will be without freshness, and to that extent without the merit of a true work of art. Work should always look as though it had been done with ease, however elaborate; what we see should appear to have been done without effort, whatever may be the agonies beneath

Opposite: Miss Eveleen Tennant, 1874

the surface. M. Meissonier surpasses all his predecessors, as well as all his contemporaries, in the quality of high finish, but what you see is evidently done easily and without labour. I remember Thackeray saying to me, concerning a certain chapter in one of his books, that the critics agreed in accusing him of carelessness, 'Careless? If I've written that chapter once I've written it a dozen times – and each time worse than the last!' – a proof that labour did not assist in his case. When an artist fails it is not so much from carelessness: to do his best is not only profitable to him, but a joy. But it is not given to every man – not, indeed, to any – to succeed whenever, and however, he tries. The best painter that ever lived never entirely succeeded more than four or five times; that is to say, no artist ever painted more than four or five *masterpieces*, however high his general average may have been, for such success depends on the coincidence, not only of genius and inspiration, but of health and mood and a hundred other mysterious contingencies. For my own part, I have often been laboured, but whatever I am I am never careless. I may honestly say that I never consciously placed an idle touch upon canvas; and that I have always been earnest and hard-working; yet the worst pictures I

Opposite: The Blind Girl, 1854-56

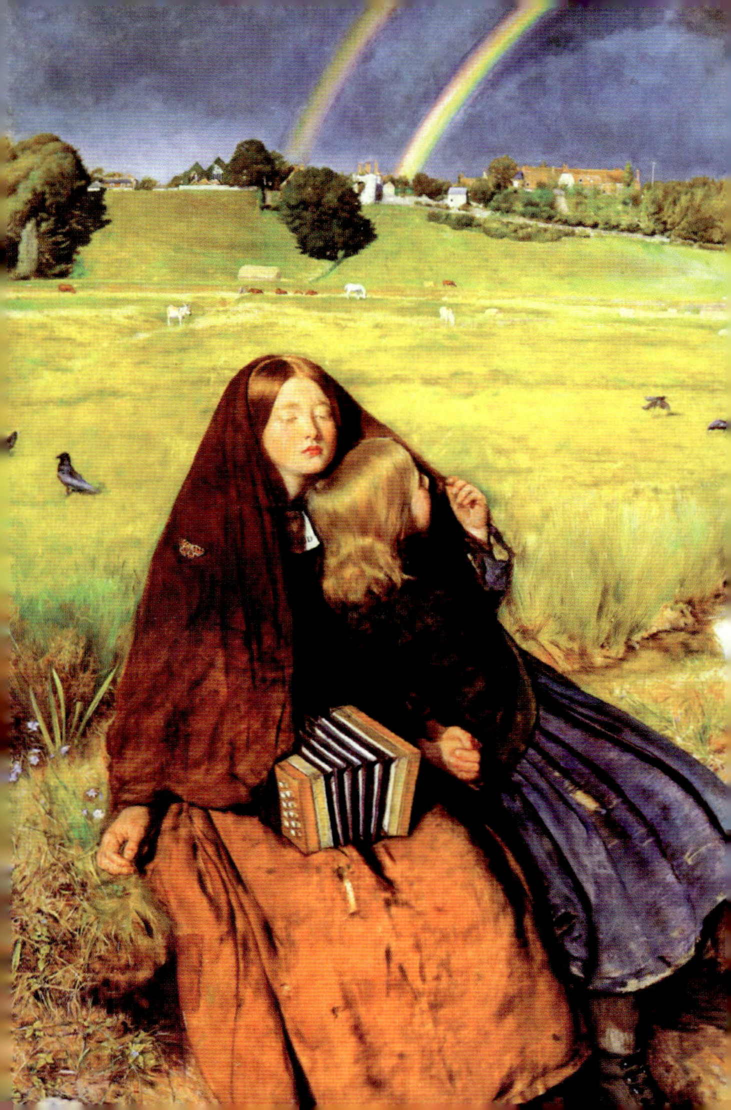

ever painted in my life are those into which I threw most trouble and labour, and I confess I should not grieve were half my works to go to the bottom of the Atlantic – if I might choose the half to go. Sometimes as I paint I may find my work becoming laborious; but as soon as I detect any evidence of that labour I paint the whole thing out without more ado.

It will be remembered that Rembrandt in his first period was very careful and minute in detail, and there is evidence of stippling in his flesh-painting; but when he grew older and in the fullness of his power, all appearance of such manipulation and minuteness vanished in the breadth and facility of his brush, though the advantage of his early manner remained. The latter manner is, of course, much the finer and really the more finished of the two. I have closely examined his pictures at the National Gallery, and have actually *seen*, beneath that grand veil of breadth, the early work that his art conceals from untrained eyes – the whole science of painting. And herein lies his superiority to Velasquez, who, with all his mighty power and magnificent execution, never rose to the perfection which, above all with painters, consists in *Ars celare Artem*.

MARION HARRY SPIELMANN

Sir John E. Millais, Bart, P. R. A.

A Sketch

1898

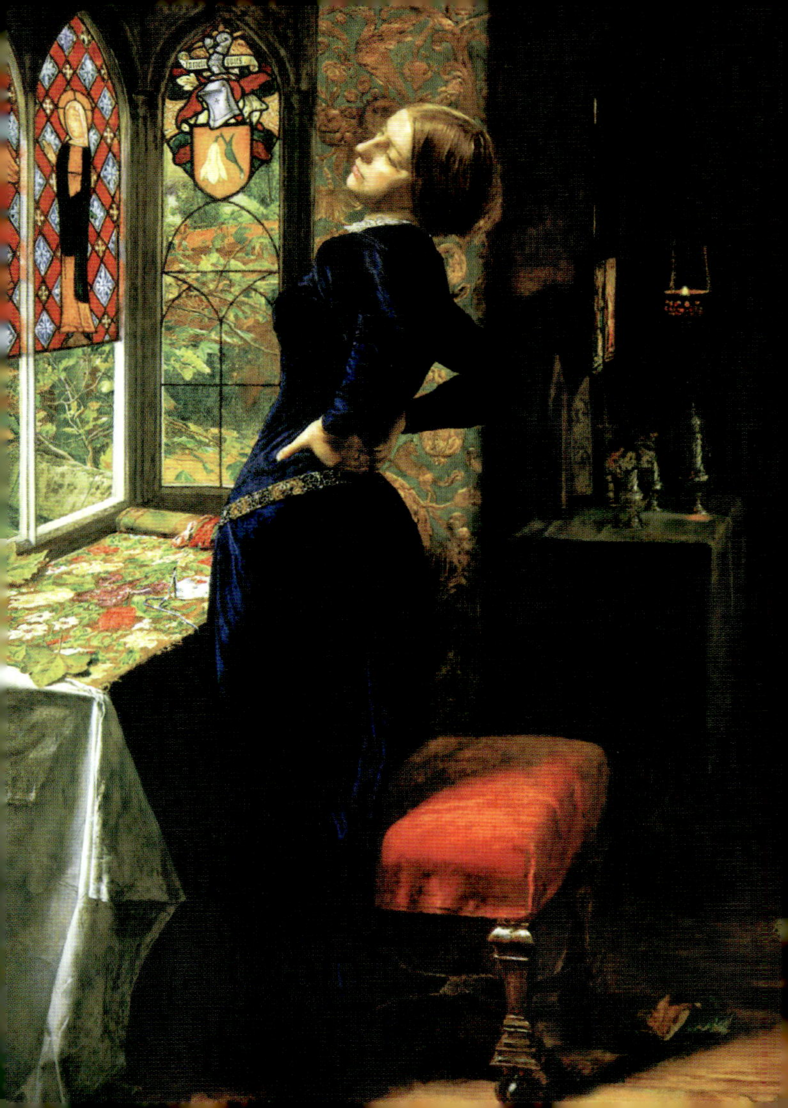

It was in the summer of 1896 that the fatal truth of the hopelessness of his malady burst with terrible suddenness upon the new President of the Royal Academy. He bore the verdict, nevertheless, with the courage, almost with the good-humour, that distinguished his fine and lofty character; and a brilliant life was snatched away leaving English art deprived of its brightest, if not its greatest, ornament. 'I always said,' were his whispered words to me as I left him for the last time, 'that Watts would outlive us both.' He was speaking of Lord Leighton's death. His words came true, sooner than we thought.

John Everett Millais was born on the 8th June, 1829, in Portland Place, Southampton, where his parents were temporarily residing. His father's was an old Jersey family that had been resident in the island for many generations – since the Conqueror's time, he said; and he added, with a genealogist's interest and with a touch of pride, that his own family and that of the French Millet – a name not uncommon on the mainland hard by – could be traced to a common ancestor. And he cherished the patriotic conviction – though he would give expression to it with a laugh – that, so far from Jersey being

Opposite: Mariana, 1850-51

a British possession, Jersey originally annexed England. Nevertheless, there was nothing French in either his demeanour, his person, or his mode of thought; indeed, to the last he knew nothing, if he ever knew aught, of the language, and when in company with French artists he would address them heartily in his own tongue, in the characteristically British hope that he would certainly make himself intelligible. 'I don't understand you and you don't understand me,' he cried jovially to Monsieur Emile Wauters on being introduced to him, 'but I'm very glad indeed to make your acquaintance!' And the two men grasped hands, and their expressive smiles, accentuated by oft-repeated nods – and what a delightful thing was Millais's smile! – were more eloquent than spoken words. He was, in fact, an uncompromising Englishman – a point on which I would insist in view of the contention urged by foreign critics that his attitude towards art was essentially a 'Latin' one: by which is roughly meant, that the painter's business is to paint, exclusive of all considerations of its subject and its interest and morality.

In 1835 the boy, while still in frocks, was taken with the rest of his family to live in Dinan in Brittany, and there his infantile talent for drawing, already strikingly revealed, exercised itself upon the romantic mediaeval architecture of the place, and more especially upon the uniforms of the military officers. Precocious talent has distinguished many of our great artists. Sir Thomas Lawrence was accounted a 'phenomenon', and astonished no one more than Sir Joshua Reynolds himself. But the genius of Millais had already declared itself at an age when the young Lawrence was a mere bungler with the pencil. No such youthful promise had ever been seen in England; in its juvenile perfection it might not inaptly be compared with that of the child Mozart. He was not more than six when his sketches were made the subject of mess-room bets – and won them; and when he was eight he gained the silver medal of the Society of Arts, to the astonishment of the Duke of Sussex, who distributed the prizes. According to the well-known story, his gratified and happy parents deemed it right to come to London and submit the child to the judgement of the President of the Royal Academy, Sir Martin Archer Shee, whose first unconsidered advice, 'Rather make him a chimney-sweep than an artist,' was quickly changed by a glance at the boy's work. When, not without difficulty, the President was persuaded that the drawings really were from the childish hand, he was struck with amazement, and warmly declared that the parents' plain duty was to bring young Millais up to the vocation for which Nature had evidently intended him. The boy was accordingly placed in the best preparatory art school of, the period – Mr. Sass's academy in Bloomsbury, afterwards Carey's – and two years later, during which time he had been diligently drawing from the cast in the British Museum, being now eleven years old, he was admitted a student of the Royal Academy. The six years that followed were passed in its schools, and there the boy carried off every prize for which he competed.

He was recognised as a marvel, and all stood astonished at his work – just as Ghirlandaio was amazed at the extraordinary skill of the young Michelangelo, and Verrocchio at the power of Leonardo da Vinci. In 1846, the seventeenth year of his age, he contributed his first picture to the Royal Academy exhibition, *Pizarro Seizing the Inca of Peru*,[1] which was selected by an eminent French critic as one of the two best historical works of the year. The canvas subsequently passed into the possession of the late Mr. H. Hodgkinson, and then into the hands of his widow. It rests, for the time, in the South Kensington Museum. In the following year he so far

[1] V&A Museum, London

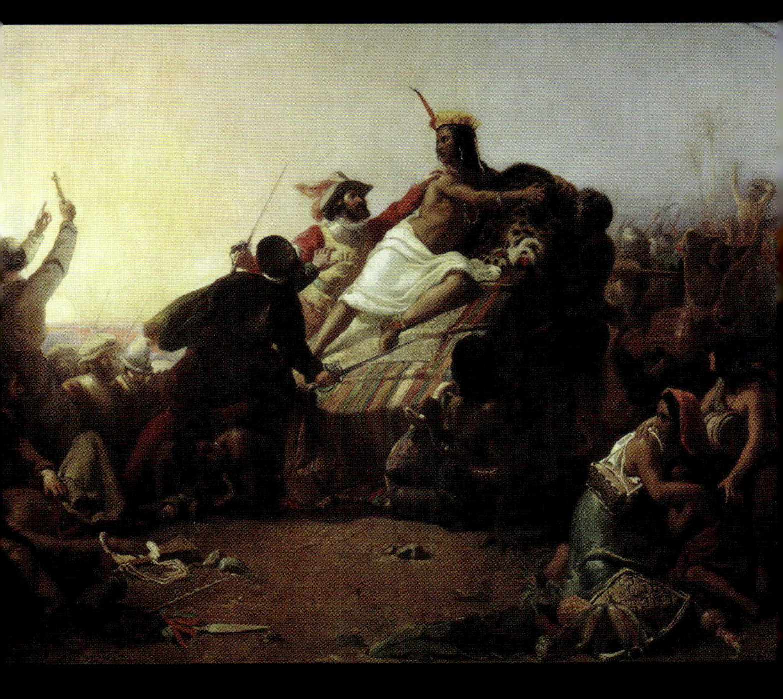

Pizarro Seizing the Inca of Peru, 1846

justified the Frenchman's belief in his powers as to carry off the gold medal for historical painting offered by the British Institution, with *The Young Men of the Destroyed Tribe of Benjamin Seizing their Destined Brides in the Vineyards*, or, as it became better known, *The Tribe of Benjamin Seizing the Daughters of Shiloh.*[1] Other works of the same year were *Elgiva Seized by Order of Archbishop Odo,*[2] an ambitious picture full of movement; and the first painting which he executed under the title of *The Widow's Mite,*[3] a cartoon of vast size sent to the famous Westminster Hall competition of 1847, to which Mr. Watts, Sir John Tenniel, Sir Noel Paton, Armitage, Cope, William Linton, Mr. Horsley, and others were successful contributors.

One of his first productions, *The Widow's Mite* is peculiarly interesting, for it shows how early appeared the religious vein, which, at intervals, the painter loved to work. It was intellectually inadequate; for in spite of the happy arrangement and composition of the work, the figure of Christ was lacking in divine dignity, just as in his latest picture, *The Forerunner* (1896),[4] the figure of St. John was, as a creative work, intellectually deficient. There was

[1] Private collection, New York [2] Private collection   [3] Later cut up, fragments in Christchurch Priory, Dorset   [4] Glasgow City Museums, Kelvingrove

48

always that impressiveness in these religious or Biblical works which belongs to manly sincerity and devotion; but they lacked the note of grandeur, when Millais was left to himself. Greatness is equally to be denied to the *Enemy Sowing Tares*,[1] for even that is strong rather from his dramatic power than from any ability to realise upon canvas the deepest passion of true religious or philosophic thought.

Yet with all his genius, with all his academical success, with all the recognition of his talents which was at last freely accorded him from many quarters, Millais's career now passed into a sombre period – an interval of ceaseless struggle, of neglect, and, when neglect was no longer possible to the public, of scorn and derision, which we who look back over his progress through a stretch of nearly half a century are apt to forget. In the dazzling brilliancy of that career we are liable to overlook the black spot which fills the vista of the past. It was an upward fight against adverse circumstances in which none ungifted with Millais's moral courage, pertinacity, and self-confidence could ever hope to win. Could he have doubted in all these trials and disappointments of the success that awaited him at last ? I hardly think so, though he himself has told me that he was not

[1] Birmingham City Art Gallery

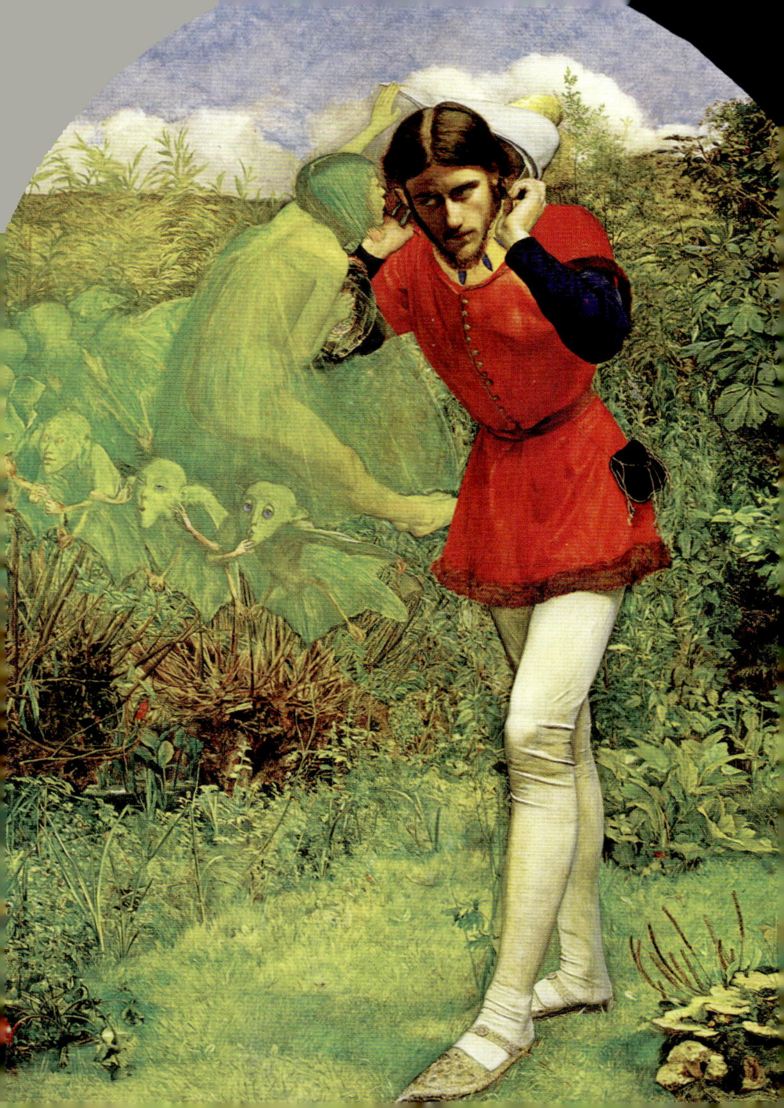

sure. His indomitable spirit and energy and his power of concentration were such as to render him famous in most walks of life.

At this period he was glad enough to make drawings of actors at ten shillings apiece, and to turn out portraits at from £2 to £3 a head. Nevertheless, the training was a good one for the crusade of the Pre-Raphaelite Brotherhood that was to follow; though even *The Carpenter's Shop*[1] was commissioned for only £150, and the *Ferdinand lured by Ariel*[2] for £100 (and returned to the painter by the dissatisfied 'patron'), while all the time these works were shaking the art world of England to its basis, and the *Times* was hurling thunderbolts of denunciation and contumely upon the head of the pachydermatous artist and his associates. Pachydermatous, perhaps; but not insensible or unconscious: courage and resolution, not indifference to attack, were his armour. *The Huguenot*,[3] too, one of his finest works, was esteemed as such by the painter; yet he was glad to sell it for £200, payable in small instalments.

'This youth will be such, to judge from what we here see, that if he lives, and should go on as he has begun, he will carry his art to the skies.' These words,

[1] Tate Gallery, London; see p. 59 [2] & [3] Makins Collection, USA

Opposite: Ferdinand lured by Ariel, 1849-50

which Raphael spoke of Jacopo da Pontormo, might well have been uttered of Millais at this time; indeed, we know that they were so applied by men who understood and applauded, though the public only scoffed. It was at this time that Millais joined with his friends Rossetti, Mr. Holman Hunt, and others of lesser artistic importance, half in fun, but really in earnest, to found, in protest against the debased generalisation of the day, that Pre-Raphaelite Brotherhood of which John Ruskin wrote (*Times*, 13th May, 1851) that he could not compliment them on common sense in the choice of a *nom de guerre*, as the principles were neither Pre- nor Post-Raphaelite, but Everlasting. This is no time to examine the principles and the bearings of this oft-discussed mission of eclectics; but it may at least be pointed out how clear a proof of what can be done by co-operation, even in art, are the achievements of the school. Millais's great pictures of that period – in many qualities really great – are certainly the combination of the influence of others' powers besides his own. His is the wonderful execution, the fine composition, the brilliant drawing; but Dante Rossetti's perfervid imagination was on one side of him, and Holman Hunt's power-

Opposite: A Huguenot on St. Bartholomew's Day, refusing to shield himself from danger by wearing the Roman Catholic badge, 1851-52

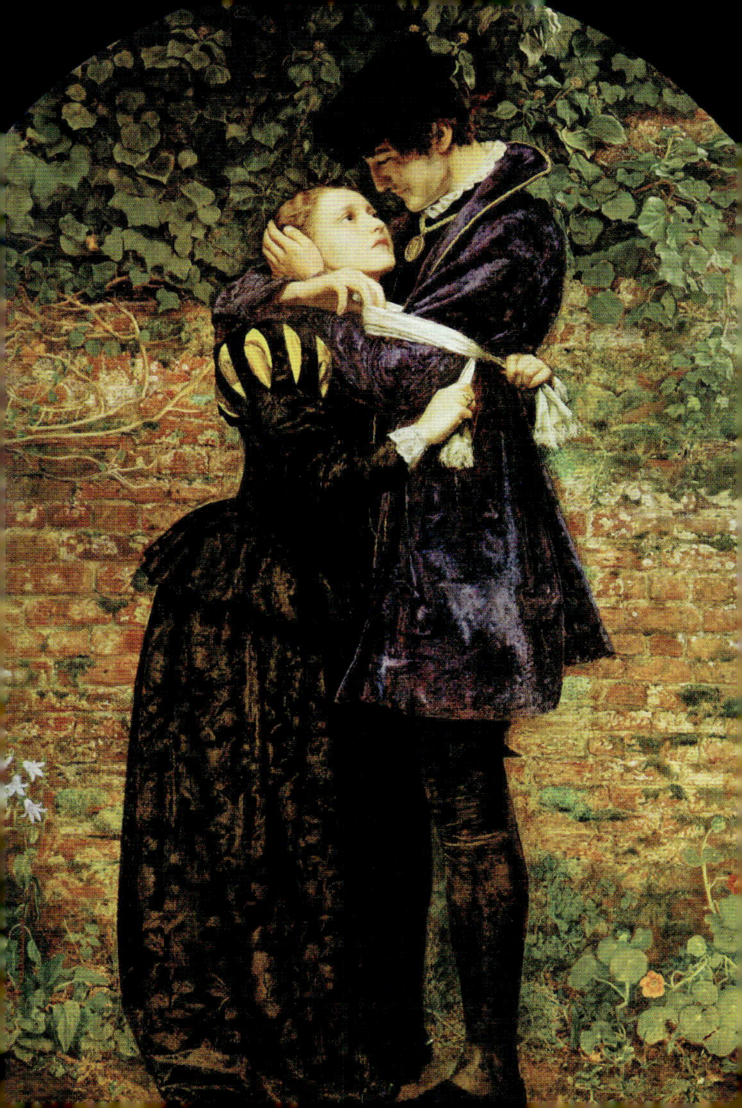

ful intellect and resolution were on the other; while perhaps the analytical mind of Mr. William Rossetti and the literary outlook of Mr. F. G. Stephens were not without influence upon his work. In a few short years these supports were withdrawn from Millais's art, in which we find the execution still, but where – at least in the same degree – the intellect or the imagination? In Holman Hunt we see a complementary effect: Dante Rossetti inspired him too, but in a lesser degree; his intellect strengthened the inspiration; and Millais's advice was there to help the execution of all three. Rossetti, on his part, had the assistance of the others' enthusiasm, but his own poetic sense was so dominant – further coloured as it was by Ford Madox Brown's personality and quaint sense of style – that there was less reflection from the others' talent in his case than in that of his friends. Though Hunt's deliberateness of mind was perhaps of some restraining influence, Millais's pre-eminence in dexterity, being a manual and material rather than an intellectual or emotional excellence, had less effect than was exerted by the others. Yet, even in Rossetti – at least in his single figures and heads – we see how he gradually emerged from the influence of Madox Brown, and passed in a measure under that of Holman Hunt. The 'Brotherhood' – which neither smoked, nor drank, nor swore, at a period when all Bohemianism was saturated with tobacco, spirits, and quaint oaths, but directed its intense enthusiasm towards things artistic and pure (though curiously enough with little sense of music) – this Brotherhood, I say, had been profoundly moved by the publication about this time of two books: the first, the set of engravings in the Campo Santo in Pisa; and the second, the superb work on costume by M. Bonnard, a collection of fine etchings by Mercuri in two volumes, which inspired the little band with immense enthusiasm. Certain of the most telling costumes in *Lorenzo and Isabella*,[1] and a little of the stiffness, too, were obtained from it.

Although himself a ringleader in this Pre-Raphaelite Brotherhood revolution, Millais was extremely intolerant of agitation for agitation's sake. When the matter of Mr. Tate's splendid offer to the nation was forming the subject of outrageous personal attacks on the intending donor and hostile agitation against the gift, Millais was recovering from influenza in Perthshire; but on the day of his return, I saw him and told him of what had been passing. He was extremely indignant. 'It was here in my dining-room,' he exclaimed, 'that Mr. Tate, Leighton, and

[1] Walker Art Gallery, Liverpool

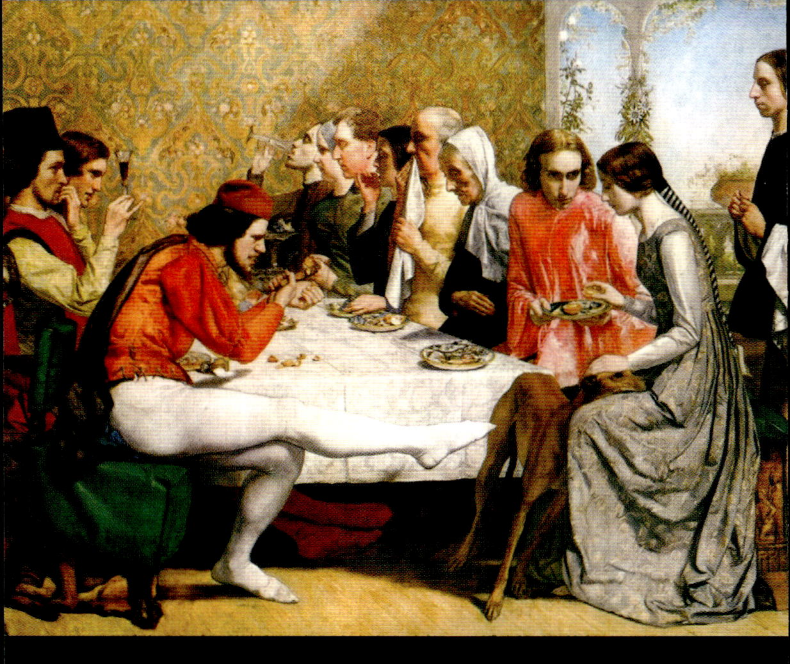

Lorenzo and Isabella
1849

Lord Carlisle met, and we talked it over and settled it as far as we could. You see the utter hopelessness of establishing anything, even for the good of the nation, when there are insolent disturbers abroad!' – an opinion he repeated in a letter later on. On another occasion when he was hotly denouncing 'agitation' and revolutionary preachers of reform, Mr. Holman Hunt, who was of the party, quietly reminded him that Christ himself had been an agitator. 'Yes,' answered Millais, warmly, 'and He got stoned! And quite right, too, from the point of view of people who saw nothing of His divinity – only His agitation. That's all I'd have seen if I'd been there; I'm afraid I'd have thrown stones, too!' Here we have a glimpse of that intense realism and vivid common-sense that made Millais so remarkable an individuality among the most illustrious of his associates.

Millais's *Lorenzo and Isabella* (1849) was the first earnest performance by this rollicking novice with the brand-new creed, which, with its realistic portraits of the artist's friends, was held to be the prime joke of the year by a dullard public, insensible alike to the astounding ability and the noble novelty of the work. It was received with even greater ridicule than Holman Hunt's *Rienzi* in the same exhibition. But in the following year ridicule turned to violent opprobrium when *The Carpenter's Shop*, otherwise known as *Christ in the House of His Parents*, was exhibited under the title of the text: 'And one shall say unto him, What are these wounds in thine hands? Then he shall answer, Those with which I was wounded in the house of my friends. (Zechariah xiii. 6.)' The *Times* – the vigorous representative of popular opinion – loudly protested. 'That morbid infatuation,' it declared, 'which sacrifices truth, beauty, and genuine feeling to mere eccentricity deserves no quarter at the hands of the public;' and the responsive public in general revolted against what they held to be fantastic in conception, outrageous in realisation, and repulsive as a whole. There were some who could appreciate the religious symbolism which was one of the principles of the Brotherhood; others, though fewer, who forgave the artist for the sake of his sincere and careful elaboration of detail; but fewest of all could see, eye to eye with the painter, how *The Carpenter's Shop* should be made like a carpenter's shop, and how realism, with eloquent symbolism enforced, could make as pious and passionate a piece of painting as the idealised grace, the picturing, and attitudinising of any of the Old Masters one may choose to name. In these hard times of struggle when notoriety rather than fame was his portion, when his

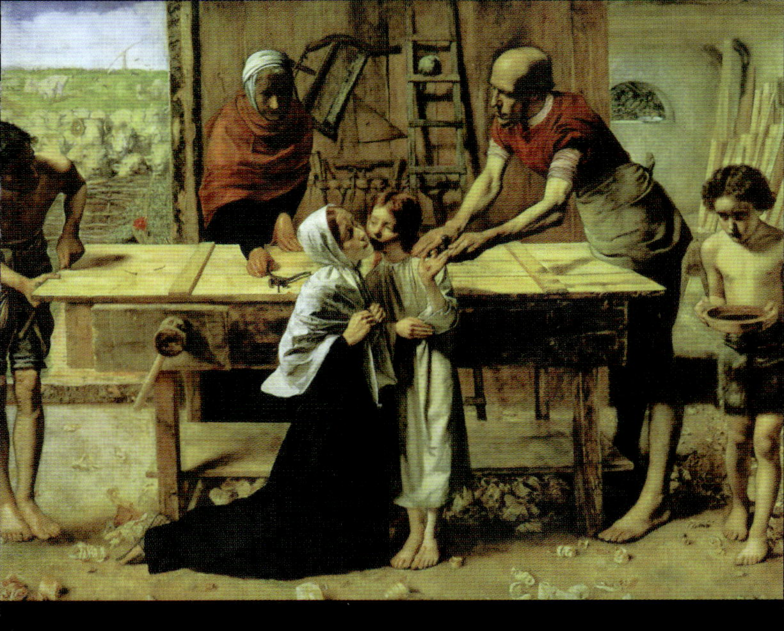

Christ in the house of his father ('The Carpenter's Shop)
1849-50

name was on many lips, for condemnation and scorn rather than for praise or honour, Millais stiffened his back, pursued his chosen path, and deserved the glory that he knew would come. 'Thackeray sympathised with me and spurred me on,' he would say, in recalling his early days, 'when I was so dreadfully bullied.' With unsurpassable courage and with the most pathetic patience he stood against the abuse and contempt of the whole world, unmoved alike by the torrents of ridicule and the withering vituperation that were rained upon the daring innovators.

Ruskin's burning championship was one of his first encouragements; the second, he told me once, was a certain bitter disappointment. He was elected an Associate of the Royal Academy, which institution, as a body, was never entirely insensible to his extraordinary merits; but when it was found that the artist had not yet arrived at the proper age for qualification, the election was quashed, and not renewed until the year 1853, when he was received into the fold – the youngest Associate, except Sir Thomas Lawrence, ever elected into the Royal Academy. But the mortification he had long endured was not complete, for he had to wait not fewer than ten years for promotion to full membership, and more than once the idea of resignation flashed across his mind; for he resented the unmerited indifference to his claims although his pictures, perhaps more than any one else's, had come to be regarded by the public as of the very first importance in the annual exhibitions they adorned.

Not till 1859, when the *Vale of Rest*[1] appeared, did Millais forswear the tenets of the Brotherhood; or, as he called it, 'emerge from his artistic puberty.' It is to be noted – as has already been suggested – that when, with the independence characteristic of his vigorous temperament, he cast off the influence of his great companions in art, Millais became, generally speaking, less of the poet and the thinker, and more of the painter and technician. But his sympathies, like his art, widened out, his range broadened in harmony with his more comprehensive interest in life; and what he lost for a time, if not altogether, in pure passion, he gained in scope. Ruskin roundly denounced his defection, which to him amounted to artistic apostasy; but Millais went calmly on amid the growing applause – for which in truth, in spite of all its sweetness, he cared not overmuch – and took the praise much as he had taken the blame that had been his portion heretofore. He had conquered his public with a concession, and was fast becoming its painter-hero.

[1] Tate Gallery, London

Yet never was it truer than in his case that the child is father to the man; so completely was his later success based upon the stern self-training both of hand and mind. For this reason, hardly one of his pictures of that period should be passed over. *Ferdinand lured by Ariel* (1850) was perhaps, with its metal gold ornament, more *quattrocento* than anything he had done. Then came *Mariana in the Moated Grange*,[1] suggested by Tennyson's poem – an example of the artist's dependence for his inventive imagination upon others, his artistic receptivity being at the same time more keenly sensitive to the emotional class of our nobler written poetry than, perhaps, any other painter of his eminence who ever appeared in England. In the same year there came the *Return of the Dove to the Ark*,[2] which was exhibited in Paris in 1855, and was bequeathed by Mr. Combe to the University of Oxford; and *The Woodman's Daughter*,[3] suggested by the poem of Coventry Patmore. In the following year *The Angel in the House*[4] was exhibited frankly as the portrait of Mrs. Coventry K. Patmore, together with the famous and ever-popular picture of *The Huguenot*. The year 1853 was rendered notable by

[1] Tate Gallery, London   [2] Ashmolean Museum, Oxford
[3] Guildhall, London   [4] Fitzwilliam Museum, Cambridge

Opposite: The Return of the Dove to the Ark, 1851

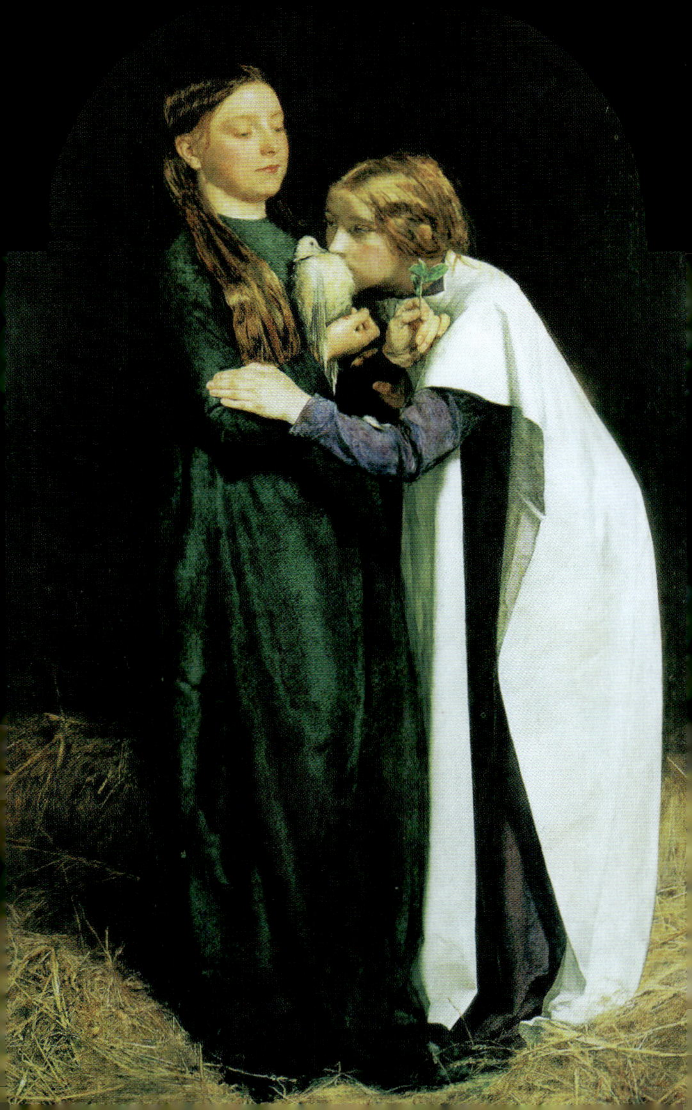

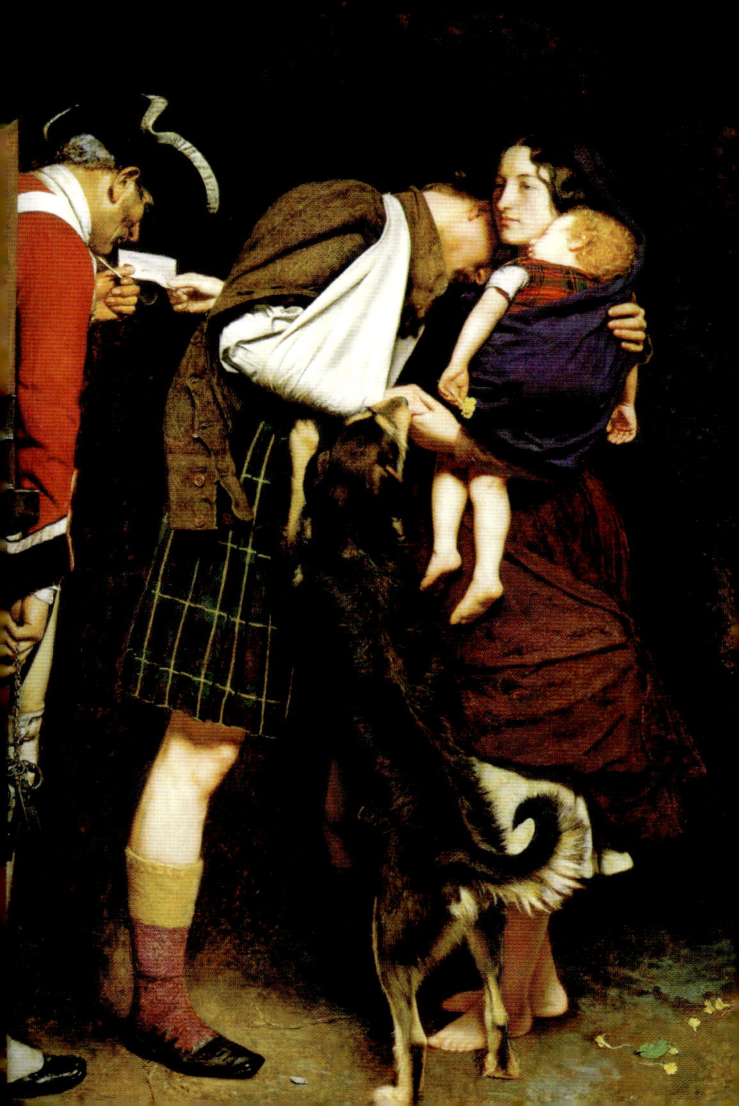

The Order of Release, 1746,[1] accompanied as it was by the hostile comment that the hero, as in the *Huguenot*, appears, awkwardly enough, to possess only one leg. Moreover, it might equally have been objected that the former picture is illogical in its drama, inasmuch as the warder has set his prisoner free before the order of release has been actually delivered and read. But in such petty objections the critics entirely missed the superlative quality of flesh-painting in this brilliant work, as well as the supreme achievement in the rendering of expression and emotion. Then there were *The Proscribed Royalist, 1651,*[2] and, above all, *Ophelia,*[3] the model for which was Miss Siddal, afterwards Dante Rossetti's wife.

In 1854 came the magnificent little portrait of Professor Ruskin standing beside the waterfall of Glenfinlas,[4] and in the following year the portrait of Mrs. John Leech,[5] and *The Rescue,*[6] which Ruskin declared to be 'the only *great* picture exhibited this year'; excusing the somewhat un-Pre-Raphaelite summariness of the handling on the ground that

[1] Tate Gallery, London [2] Lloyd Webber Collection, Sydmonton
[3] Tate Gallery, London   [4] Private Collection, East Sussex
[5] Private collection [6] National Gallery of Victoria, Melbourne

Opposite: The Order of Release – 1746, 1852-3

there is a true sympathy between the impetuousness of execution and the haste of the action represented. In *Peace Concluded, 1856*[1] – (which appeared in that year, and of which Ruskin enthusiastically exclaimed: 'Titian himself could hardly head him now. This picture is as brilliant in invention as consummate in executive power; both this and *Autumn Leaves*[2] will rank in future among the world's best masterpieces')– in this canvas there is the symbolism, a little puerile perhaps, dear at that time to the Pre-Raphaelite heart for in the very toys with which the children play, the lion, the cock, and the bear, in their respective attitudes, we are given a sort of political *résumé* of the Crimean War. *Autumn Leaves*, which was originally painted for Mr. Eden, was rightly declared by the great critic to be the first instance existing of perfectly painted twilight. In addition to these, there were *L'Enfant du Régiment*, now called *The Random Shot*,[3] another little piece of tender drama *Pot Pourri*,[4] for which Mrs. Stibbard, the artist's sister-in-law, when Miss Gray, sat for the principal of the two little girls, and *The Blind Girl*,[5] in which the scene, by the way, is

[1] Minneapolis Institute of Arts   [2] City Art Gallery, Manchester; see p. 2 [3] Yale Center for British Art, New Haven [4] Private collection [5] Birmingham City Museums; see p. 39

Opposite: Peace Concluded – 1856, 1856

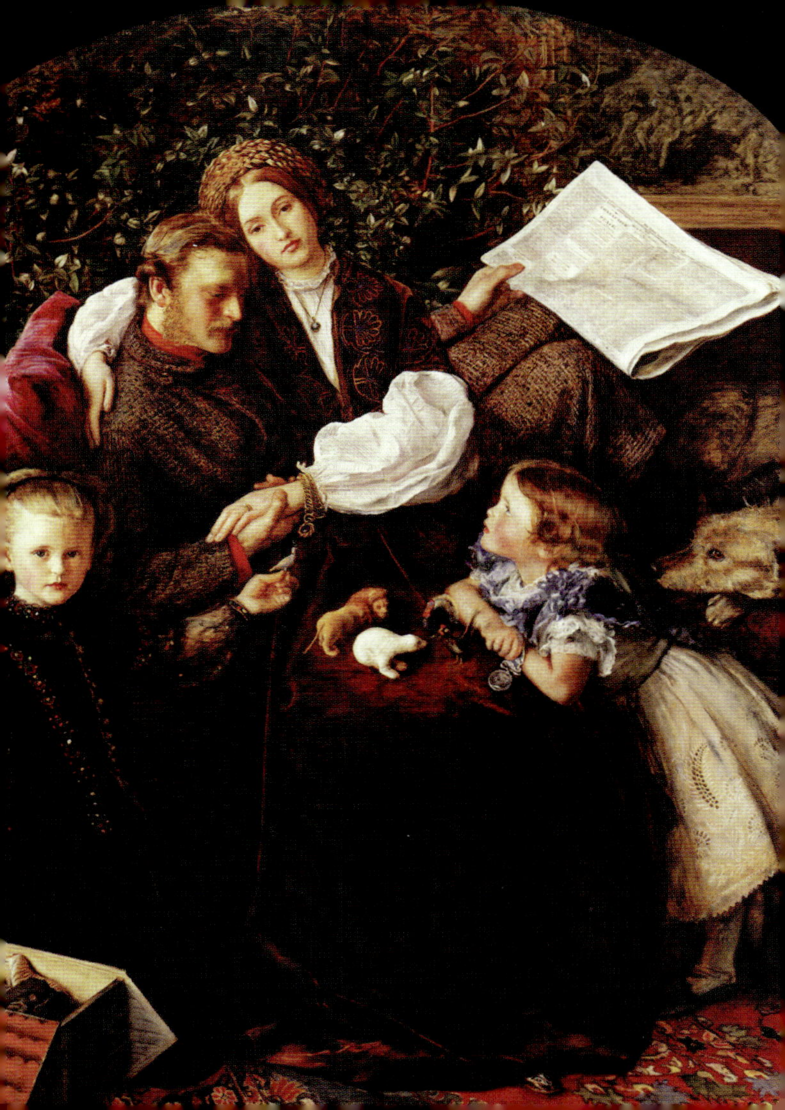

a Winchelsea landscape, with the quaint episode of the double rainbow (to emphasise thereby, together with the gorgeous death's-head butterfly, the full affliction of loss of sight and the supreme consolation of the Divine promise); and the reader who acquaints himself with the extreme conscientiousness of finish lavished upon these works will form a conception of the feverish industry of the painter. Then, in 1857, there came *A Dream of the Past – Sir Isumbras at the Ford*,[1] *News from Home*,[2] and *The Escape of a Heretic, 1559*,[3] suggested by official documents in Valladolid relating to the Inquisition.

This, so far as the Pre-Raphaelite Brotherhood was concerned, was the beginning of the end. Ruskin detected in *Sir Isumbras* faults of fact, of sentiment, and of art; while in *The Escape* he saw the everlasting seal placed by Pre-Raphaelite hands themselves upon their acceptance of the charge of a special love for ugliness which had always been flung at them by the public, and for which the writer could, for once, find no excuse. The fact was that Millais, who would listen to no public, now proclaimed by his brush that he would listen to no adviser, not even to Ruskin; and since that time he declared more than once in my

[1] Lady Lever Art Gallery, Port Sunlight [2] Walters Art Gallery, Baltimore [3] Museo de Arte, Ponce, Puerto Rico

hearing that, let his judges think what they might, his decade of Pre-Raphaelitism rather hindered than helped his development and his art. The year 1858 was a fallow season, for which Ruskin duly scolded, while Mr. Frith's *Derby Day* drew the town. But the following year was rendered notable by the great transition. The *Apple-blossoms*,[1] exhibited under the name of *Spring*, offended by its 'fierce and rigid orchard' and by 'the angry blooming' of its marvellously painted flowers; while *The Love of James I of Scotland*[2] was little noticed under the tumult of criticism and protest which met the *Vale of Rest*. The last-named picture I have always felt to be one of the greatest and most impressive ever painted in England; one in which the sentiment is not mawkish nor the tragedy melodramatic – a picture, indeed, to look at with hushed voice and bowed head; in which the execution is not overwhelmed by the story; nor the story otherwise than emphasised by the composition; and in which the composition is worthy of the handling. 'Year Mr. Millais gave forth those terrible nuns in the graveyard' – thus 'Mr. Punch' characterised the year 1859. Even Ruskin, denouncing the methods, and admitting, unjustly, as it now appears after the re-painting, the ugliness and 'frightfulness'

[1] Lady Lever Art Gallery, Port Sunlight [2] Private collection

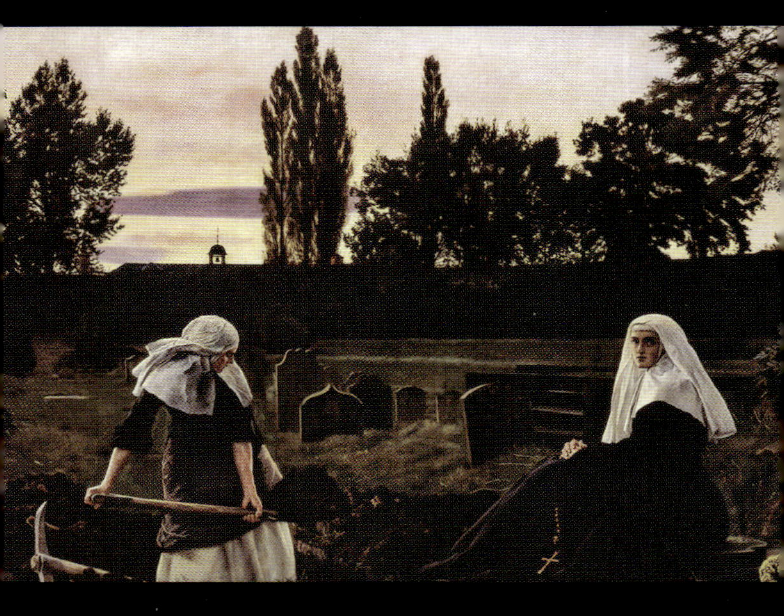

The Vale of Rest – 'Where the weary find repose'
1858

of the figures, was constrained to allow it nobility of horror if horror it was, and the greatness and profundity of the touching sentiment. His charge of crudeness in the painting no longer holds good. Time – that great Old Master to which Millais did homage in act and word – has accomplished the work the artist intended him to do, and it may truly be said that in the new National Gallery of British Art there hangs no more impressive, no more powerful, work than that which shocked the art world of 1859, and proclaimed the secession of the painter from the sectarianism of a few – that Millais had done with the persecution of an unappreciative majority.

I have dwelt at so great a length upon the early period of Millais's career because, as I have said, I believe that the attempt to avoid the affectations of more sophisticated artistic times – a movement which, by the way, had already in a manner been attempted in Germany – and to establish a Protestant artistic creed, not only permitted him to display his liberty of conscience, his hatred of conventionalism, his originality of thought, and, above all, the consciousness of his power, but also to form his character while it trained his hand. Even opponents admitted his inherent sense of style, and respected his incomparable ability, and came at last to see that the school of which he was recognised as a fountain-head and leader was influencing for good the young artistic generation, and, furthermore, was educating the general public who had not yet the wit to appreciate.

To follow the artist through his works would in this chapter be unnecessary. To select even the most notable for special mention would be difficult enough; for during a long series of years Millais's painting maintained an astonishing consistency of excellence, and the circumstance of its occasional failure is almost as interesting, noteworthy, and instructive as the oft-repeated success. Nor is it the high level of attainment which constitutes his only, or, indeed, his chief claim to the position he conquered; it was the universality of his genius in every section of the pictorial arts. He was a dramatist, with the true artist's instinct of leaving his story unfinished, though usually suggested; his management of colour was unsurpassed in England; his drawing was irreproachable – subtle, and suggestive, as well as correct and firm; his line and composition were almost inspired; his black-and-white has never been

Opposite: Trust Me, 1862

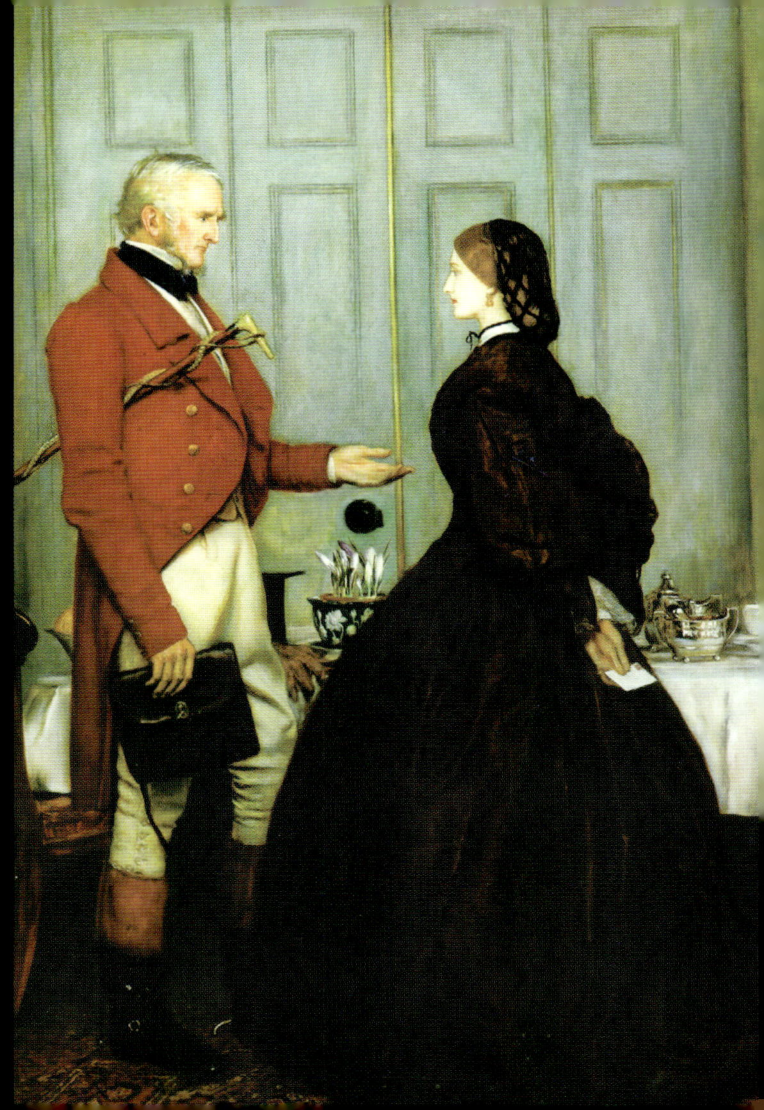

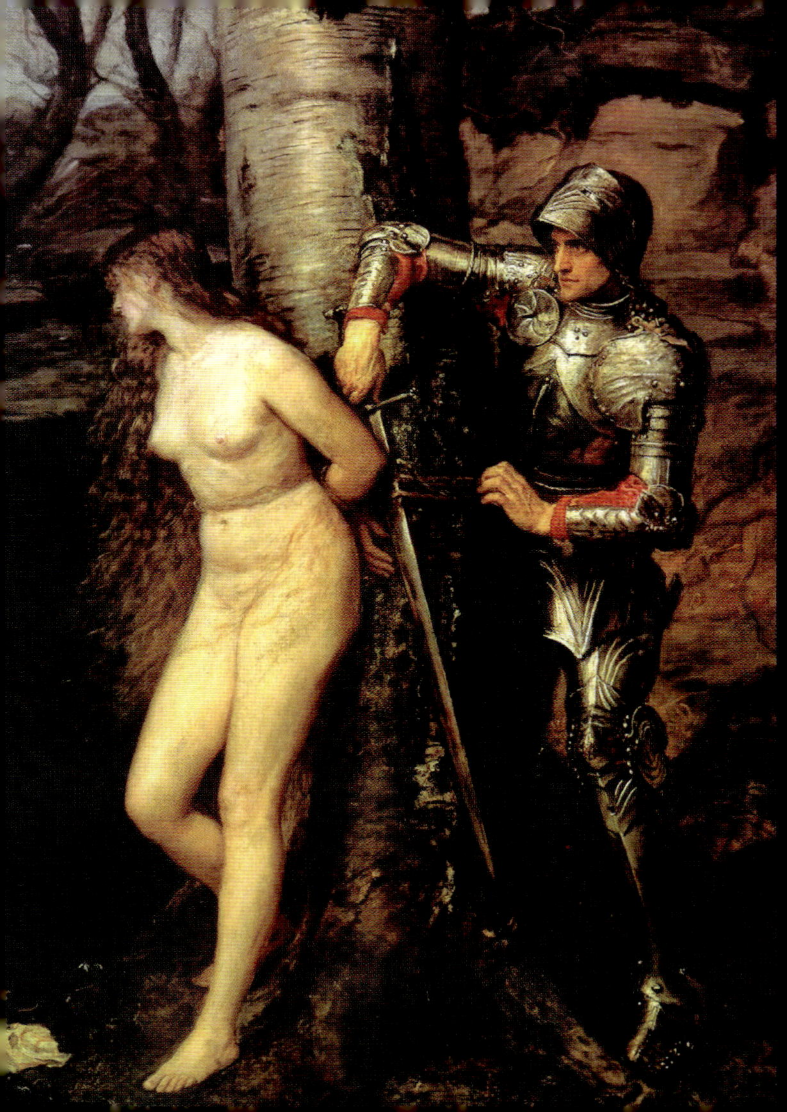

excelled; and his water-colour – in the skilful use of wash, at least – was adequate. Of his hand and materials he was the accomplished master. But more than this must be accorded him. In portraiture, in the representation of landscape, in flower painting, as well as in simple drama – for his tragedy, as in *Mercy: St. Bartholomew's Day*,[1] has almost been known to descend to melodrama, if not to bathos – in all four he has been supreme. Sympathy with the sea was almost wholly lacking: not that he could not paint water, as, if proof were needed, *A Flood* (1870),[2] *The Sound of Many Waters* (1877),[3] and *Flowing to the Sea* (1872)[4] would testify. The female nude he painted once, and only once, in *The Knight-Errant* (1870),[5] but well enough to give reason for regret that he restrained his brush in this direction. Religious or Biblical painting he indulged in from time to time with originality and sincerity, if not with the high poetical and intellectual insight we demand in such work. But Millais' imagination and invention were not equal to his transcendent powers of brilliant execution, though they could aspire to the illustration of poems in which

[1] Tate Gallery, London   [2] Manchester Art Gallery   [3] Fyvie Castle, Aberdeenshire   [4] Southampton Art Gallery [5]   Tate Gallery, London

Opposite: The Knight Errant, 1870

delicacy, grace, sweetness, and even passion were required; as in *The Eve of St. Agnes* (1863),[1] after Keats; *Swallow! Swallow!* (1865),[2] after Tennyson's *Princess*; *Oh, that a dream so long enjoyed* (1872),[3] suggested by *Lalla Rookh*, and *Pippa* (1885),[4] it may be said with less certainty, after Browning's *Pippa Passes*. Still more noticeable is this talent when the poem deals with landscape rather than with incident, as in *Scotch Firs* (1874),[5] which is illustrative of Wordsworth's line, 'The silence that is in the lonely wood;' or, *The Deserted Garden* (1875),[6] of Campbell's verse beginning, 'Yet wandering, I found in my ruinous walk' – a picture that extorted some of Ruskin's most eloquent denunciation, and which, in the rendering of flower and weed and undergrowth, challenges in the most amazingly different manner the *Ophelia*, for example, of twenty odd years before.

As a landscape-painter – that is to say, as the portrait-painter of landscape – Millais can assuredly, be compared, with loss neither of dignity nor place, with the great masters, living and dead. I do not mean to compare him with Turner in the combined glory of artistic knowledge and science of landscape, as I would call it, as well as in the magic of the

[1] Royal Collection [2] Private collection   [3] Private collection
[4] Private collection   [5] Private collection   [6] Unlocated

romantic palette, or with the artist-poet who dips at will into Nature's secrets, and reveals her emotions to the world. But as a respectful translator of an actual view, painted simply as it stands – as the mournful *Chill October*,[1] or *Murthly Moss*,[2] a joyous, luminous rendering of a scene not less difficult to handle – Millais has had no superior in this country. So great, indeed, was his first landscape that those who remembered the manner of his earlier works, and forgot the poetry of others such as *Autumn Leaves*, set down the sentiment of *Chill October* to lucky chance. Millais, so to say, could paint the time of day; he could, moreover, draw a tree as few of his contemporaries could do it; and sky and grass and dew-drenched heather, luminous screen of cloud and tangled undergrowth – he painted them all not only with love, but with an enthusiasm which he had the happy faculty of imparting to the spectator.

It is not only subtlety of eye that made Millais a great colourist; it was the skill with which, as in the *Yeoman of the Guard* (1877),[3] he would accomplish a *tour de force* with a blaze of red and gold as if it were the most natural thing in the world; harmonise the lake and scarlet of a college gown, as in the second

[1] Lloyd Webber Collection, Sydmonton; see pp. 18-19
[2] Unlocated [3] Tate Gallery, London

Gladstone portrait (1885), now at Christ Church, Oxford;[1] or place spots of violent colour in the middle of a relatively sober picture, as in *The Ornithologist* (1885),[2] so that they quietly take their place and delight the grateful eye. He was a colourist, not so much by selection as by his power of forcing the colours before him into harmony.

In estimating the place of Millais in the roll of England's painters, in judging of the services he has rendered to her art, appreciation must be accorded to the foremost position he took in the creation of that great black-and-white art which today satisfies the picture-hunger of the nation more completely and thoroughly than the more elaborate arts of painting and sculpture could hope to do, or ever did. He it was who demanded, and obtained, that finer wood-cutting which enabled Mr. Holman Hunt, Fred Walker, Rossetti, Houghton, Charles Keene, and the rest of their fellows, to draw their masterpieces more as they chose upon the block; so that not only did he, the greatest of them all, head the band of the newly-emancipated school of wood-draughtsmen of the 'sixties (for his draughtsmanship was more brilliant and suggestive than even that of Fred Walker himself), but by the force of his genius and his persistent

[1] Still in situ   [3] Glasgow City Museums, Kelvingrove

78

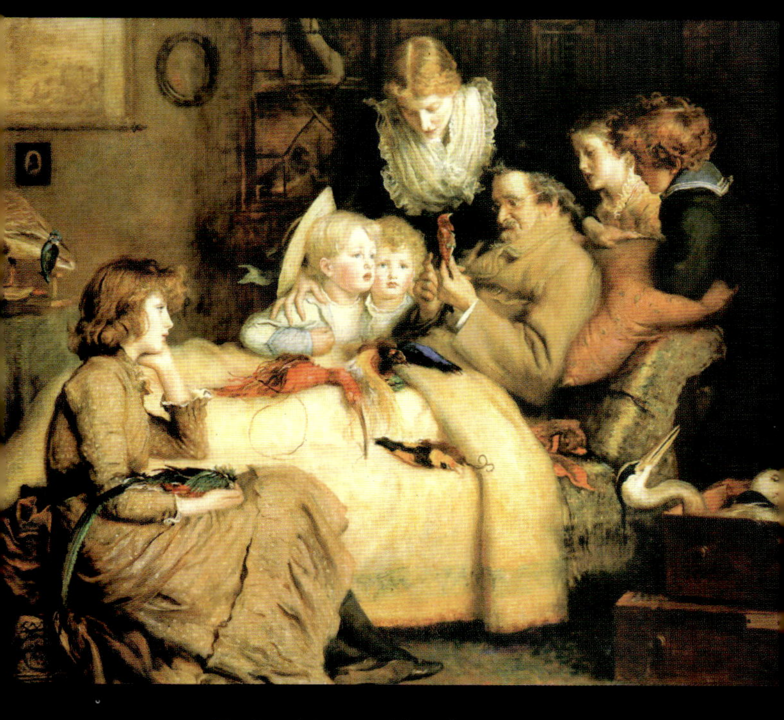

The Ornithologist, or, The Ruling Passion
1885

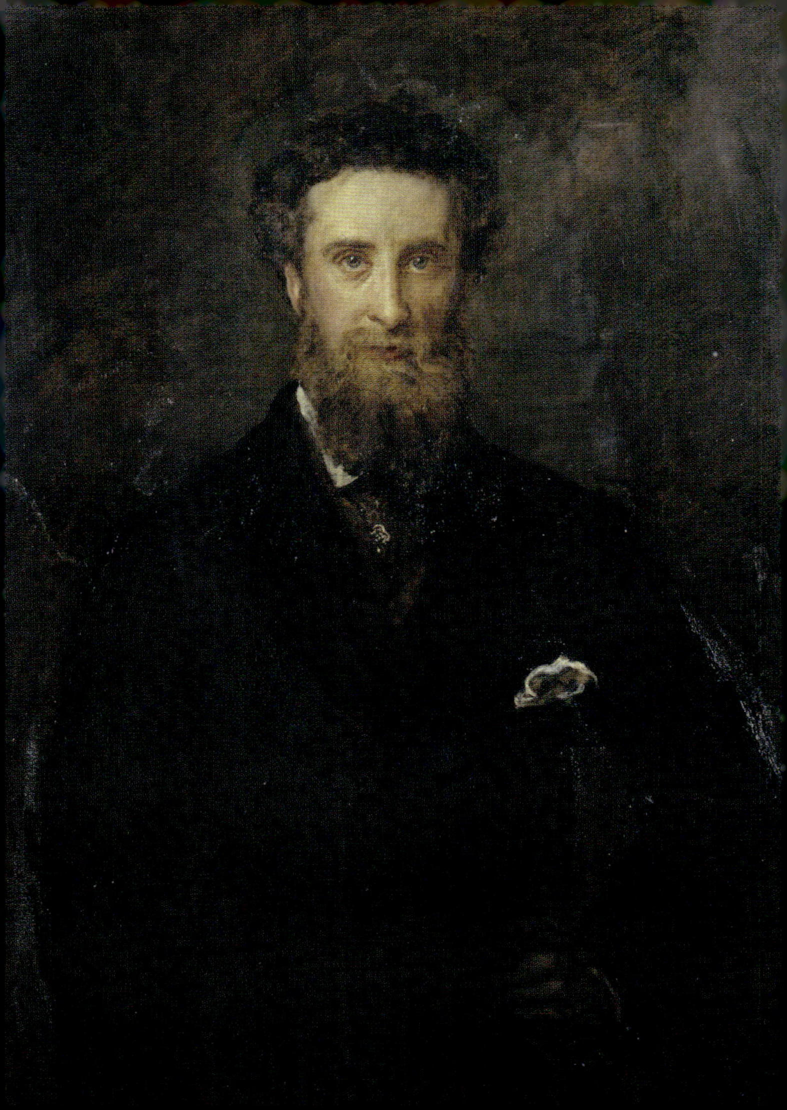

individuality he helped to revolutionise the art and craft of wood-cutting. It was he who drew attention to the fine work being accomplished abroad by Menzel, Meissonier, and a little later, by Alphonse de Neuville; he who by his work in *Once a Week* and in the *Cornhill* (especially *Orley Farm*), set a noble example nobly followed; he who pleaded with the Royal Commission for a recommendation to the Royal Academy to admit workers in black-and-white to Academical honours. It was justice he pleaded for; the cause was very near his heart, for – a thing somewhat unusual in a born colourist – his love for black-and-white was deep; and had he lived he would, as he told me, have striven hard to bring the Academy to his own enlightened view. The Academy, it may thus be seen, is not alone in having bitter cause to mourn his death.

As a portraitist Millais was in his own line supreme. He had not, perhaps, the mere technical dexterity of a few whom I could name – not the astonishing 'sleight-of-hand,' as some would call it, which, while it amazes us and extorts our admiration, makes us feel that it is not, after all, the greatest or the most desirable quality in great portraiture. But he

Opposite: Edward Bulwer-Lytton, (Lord Lytton), 1876

had the noble power of making his sitters live and breathe, of making their flesh like flesh, their eyes like eyes, with a living intelligence burning in them, if not always with a strong mind or soul behind. They were posed naturally, painted firmly, the arrangement unconventional and original and wholly dignified, pictures worthy to take and hold their place among any series of similar works from any hand whatever. Were I asked to select the finest of his male portraits, I should point, I think, to the first *Gladstone* (1879),[1] to the *Lord Tennyson* (1881),[2] *J. C. Hook, R. A.* (1883),[3] and *Sir Gilbert Greenall* (1881);[4] while of his female portraits I should choose his *Mrs. Bischoffsheim* (1873),[5] and *Mrs. Heugh* (1872).[6] In portraits of men he showed not very much imagination, save occasionally when, with great sitters, he rose characteristically to the occasion; not very much more in those of women. But the note he struck was always just, even to the end, when now and again he would produce a work unworthy of his brush; for though eye, and even hand, might play him false, there was always the Man behind them that proclaimed the mastery that had failed.

[1] National Portrait Gallery, London   [2] Lady Lever Art Gallery, Port Sunlight   [3] Private collection   [4] Private collection   [5] Tate Gallery, London   [6] Musée d'Orsay, Paris

Millais's method of work was simple and classic enough. When painting a portrait he would place the canvas beside the sitter, making no charcoal sketch nor other indication, and paint right on to the white canvas, 'matching' the colours touch by touch, constantly stepping back to test the accuracy of his work. This system was doubtless the outcome of the extremely precise and microscopic work of his youth. When painting landscape, his practice was to erect a temporary studio – a hut with front and roof of glass – facing the view he had selected for his picture, and therein would combine the advantages of studio comfort and open-air effect.

His success as a portrait-painter was never for a moment in doubt after the year 1856, when he painted one of the very few of his pictorial jokes. This is the *Portrait of a Gentleman* (the property of Mr. Chetwynd Stapylton),[1] which consists of the likeness of a boy of tender years. In due time his singular power was universally recognised, and he shared, with Mr. Watts, the position of the most fashionable and favourite portrait-painter of the day. When the latter withdrew from accepting commissions and devoted himself to the painting of his great

[1] Unlocated

intellectual works, Millais divided with Holl, and later with Mr. Ouless and Professor Herkomer, the limning of the great ones of the land; but he never surrendered his premier position. So great was the demand for his brush that it is said he would receive as much as £1,500 or even £2,000 for a portrait. To the most famous canvases in this section of his art some allusion has already been made; but the fullest list does not exhaust the number of portraits he paint-ed, in-asmuch as many of them are what are known as 'fancy-' or subject-portraits. Such, for example, are the portraits of his daughter Effie, now Mrs. James, as seen in *My First Sermon* (1863),[1] *My Second Sermon* (1864),[2] *Waking*[3] and *The Minuet* (1867),[4] and *New-Laid Eggs* (1873);[5] of his other daughter, Alice Caroline, in *Sleeping* (1867)[6] and *The Picture of Health* (1874);[7] while *Sisters*[8] include the three daughters, Mary, Caroline, and Effie; and these ladies have been once more immortalised in *Forbidden Fruit* (1876),[9] and *The Last Rose of Summer* (1888).[10] Then Miss Beatrice

[1] & [2] Guildhall Art Gallery, London [3] Perth City Art Gallery
[4] Elton Hall Collection [5] Private collection [6] Private collection
[7] Private collection [8] Private collection [9] Private collection
[10] Geoffroy Everett Richard Millais collection

Opposite: My Second Sermon (watercolour version), 1864

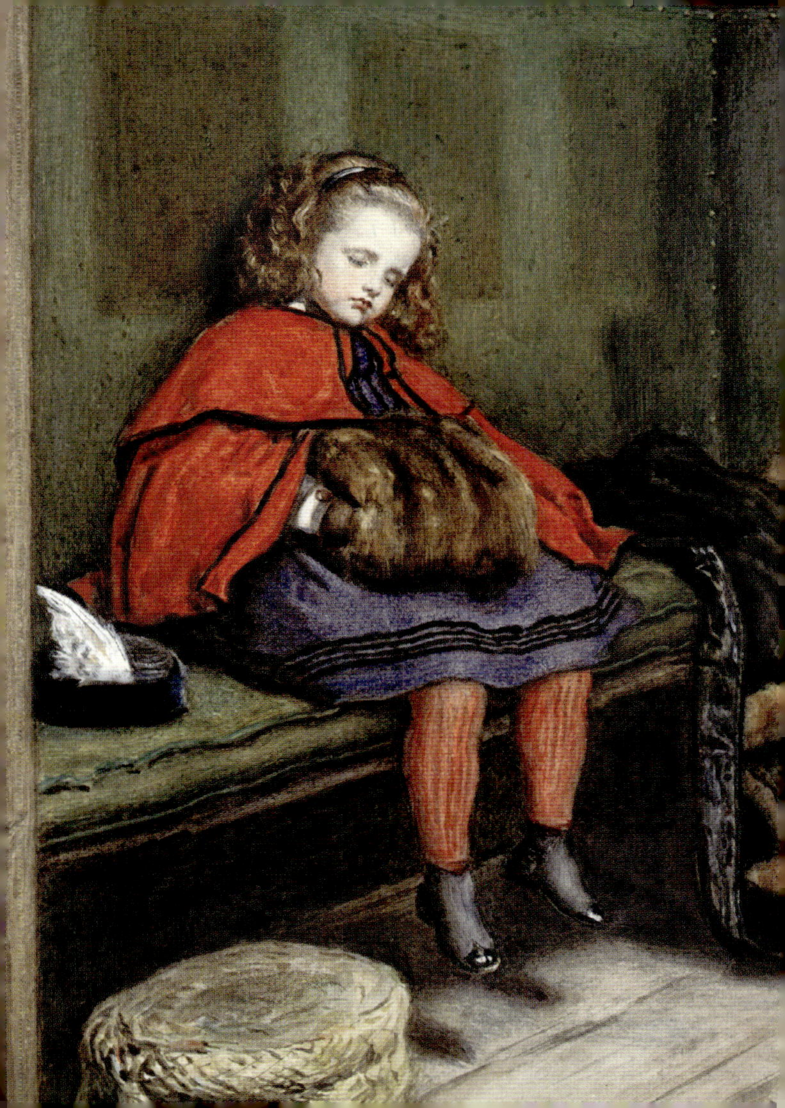

Buckstone, daughter of the comedian, sat in 1881 for the three famous pictures, *Cinderella*,[1] *Sweetest Eyes were ever Seen*,[2] and *Caller Herrin'*[3] – the last-named containing the broadest piece of Pre-Raphaelite painting he had indulged in for five-and-twenty years. Besides these, there were, in 1882, *The Captive*,[4] which was Miss Ruby Streatfield, and *Cherry Ripe*,[5] Miss Edie Ramage, though the honour has been claimed for a model, Miss Barrette; and the list might be indefinitely prolonged were more examples wanted.

It is persistently, urged in some quarters that Millais 'played to the crowd' when he composed his little dramas and devised the pictures of pretty childhood, which the public so loudly applauded. Sir John was perfectly sincere in his subjects, and by them may be estimated both his weakness and his strength. 'If I wanted to paint a "popular" picture,' he once exclaimed, 'I should paint an old man in spectacles, reading his Bible by the fireside; and the fire would be reflected on his spectacles. And I should paint a tear running down by his nose; and the fire would be reflected in the tear. That would be a 'popular' picture, I can tell you!' That that picture was never painted

[1] Lloyd Webber collection, Sydmonton   [2] National Gallery of Scotland, Edinburgh [3] Private collection [4] Art Gallery of New South Wales   [5] Private collection

must surely be accounted to him for righteousness.

It is impossible to deny that up to that fatal moment when influenza first nourished his dread disease, Millais had had in fullest measure his reward – such reward as is reserved for the magicians of the brush – even while he was still in the full prime and vigour of his manhood. He was but in his fifth year when

Genius fluttering by touched the infant with her wing –
Dropped the feather for a brush that made a painter-king,

and from that day he never really loosened his strong tenacious grip, use his talent as he might. He had followed the dictates of his artistic soul, deaf alike to public's jeers and critics' onslaughts; and indifferent, too, to the more concrete arguments of an empty purse. At last, as in the happy development of a story-book, honours and riches came to him unstinted. But far dearer to him than these – more valued by him, I know, than all else – were the pride of his countrymen and the applause of all the world. Not less was the enthusiastic love his fellow-workers bore him; and deepest down in his heart was the quiet conviction that posterity would endorse what contemporary criticism now proclaimed. This was his pride and consolation, the joy of the truly great painter who could gauge without affected humility the merit of his own work. Yet no one was ever more severe on his inferior achievements than himself – when he found it out. In 1886, when there was the great exhibition of his works at the Grosvenor Gallery (insured for a quarter of a million sterling, I was assured, though not many more than half his pictures had been collected), he arrived late at Lord Leighton's house to dine with others of the then President's friends. 'Quick!' he exclaimed, in an exhausted tone, 'give me some champagne – I'm quite ill.' Then, after a draught, he added, 'I've been seeing all my old work! – all my past misdeeds have been rising up against me! Oh, the *vulgarity* of some of them, my dear fellow! The vulgarity! *But some fine things mind you!*' He was not aware that 'vulgarity' was perhaps the worst-chosen word of any to apply to his work, whatever his failure might be.

When on the same occasion he declared – what he afterwards printed – that he would like half his pictures to go to the bottom of the Atlantic 'if he might choose the half to go,' he referred to those which had given him the most worry in their production; for it is undoubtedly the fact that his admitted failures since his Pre-Raphaelite period are precisely those on which he spent most time and trouble. He has told me so a dozen times. 'I've painted good pictures and bad ones, too; but the bad ones have invariably cost me more time and pains than the good ones. I have never knowingly left a picture as finished which I thought I could improve by more work. If only people would remember that to the painter who knows his business there are few things easier than to impart an appearance of high finish and truthfulness of imitation!' No artist I have known – not even M. Gérôme, who, nevertheless, can be very correctly hard upon himself – could judge more freshly and dispassionately of his own work, and speak of it more frankly, whether for good or evil. But not just when it was painted – a little time had to elapse. So he would call in Mr. Wells, R.A., or some other of the painter-friends whom he called his 'artistic father-confessors,' to point out the faults that might exist in his newly-painted pictures. Such faults are usually only too apparent, though in some cases almost lost in the brilliancy of the merits about them. In Leighton's case it is hard to foretell the verdict of the future – whether his artistic place will be higher or lower than we are now disposed to fix it. In Millais's, I think, there need be little doubt; for when, in time to come, men of a future generation stand in the Cathedral of St. Paul's beside these two life-long friends whose graves are head to foot, they will point to them, the one as the greatest President, the other as the greatest painter, with whom Britain has been endowed since their mighty neighbour and predecessor – the master of them both, Sir Joshua Reynolds – lived and worked and died.

Such was Sir John Millais – heartiest, honestest, kindliest among all English gentlemen of his day. He was the big man with the warm heart, which he wore upon his sleeve; plain-spoken, straightforward, genial, and affectionate, who rarely said a cruel thing and never did a harsh one; without a grain of affectation and without a touch of jealousy. Almost to the end his life upon the moors seemed to have kept him for ever young, and their winds to have blown the cobwebs of prejudice from his mind, and every morbid and paltry feeling from his heart. Unspoilt by the extraordinary measure of the well-merited success that attended the development of his genius, he maintained to the last the hearty innocence of a youth, and the high hopes and sanguine optimism of a man at the beginning of life rather than one in the prime and vigour of his later manhood, in the heyday of his fame. The death of Leighton overpowered the nation in the intellectual love they bore him; the

Opposite: Dew-Drenched Furze, 1889-90

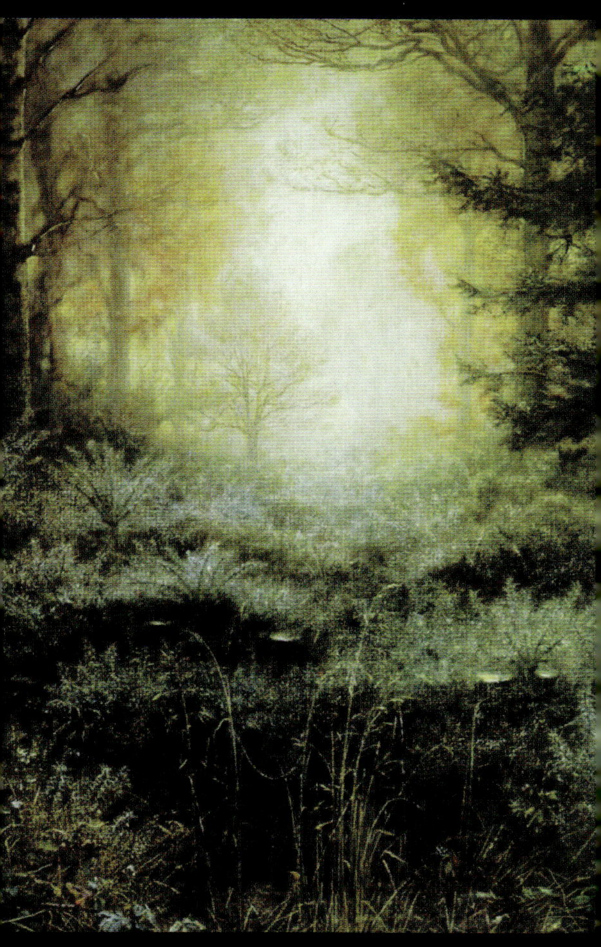

death of Millais plunged us into still profounder grief. We have not had in his case, as in Leighton's, to wait until he died to know how much we loved him. To all he thought worthy of his friendship he gave it unasked, freely and heartily, and something more than friendship came in that warm clasp of the hand, so quick to grip, so slow to loosen. So thoroughly did the greatness of the man match the greatness of the artist – such was his simplicity – that those who knew him mourned in him rather the friend whom they loved than the painter they honoured and admired.

There is little need here to recall the splendid personality of the artist – the keen sportsman, whose prowess with the gun, the rod, and the long putting cleek, and whose spirits, whether in the saddle or on foot, commanded the admiration of the many for whom the triumphs of art are a lesser achievement. But as I write, his figure seems to rise before me, shedding that magnetic pleasure round him his presence always brought. He turns to look at me, as he has done a score of times, from his round-backed chair before the great fireplace of the studio. He has discussed the pictures on the easels, ranged twice across the room, in his half-halting, half-explosive, wholly delightful way. His pipe is between his teeth – the beloved briar, more precious than the finest cigar

Havana ever rolled. The travelling-cap of tweed, at first raised once or twice as if to ventilate the head, then carelessly replaced, rakishly on one side, is finally thrown on to the table close at hand, and reveals the silver fringing to the splendid head – a hairy nimbus, like a laurel-wreath, lovingly placed by the crowning hand of Time. The strong voice – that was to become, alas, weazened, husky, and inaudible at last – sounds loud and fresh and hearty in my ears; the powerful, kindly hand is placed with genial roughness on my shoulder; the smile, so full of charm; the untutored, halting eloquence; the bright, happy, infectious roguery of the accentuating wink; the enthusiastic talk on art, now optimistic, now denunciatory of fads and foolishness; a great jolly Englishman, unaffected as a schoolboy, and as unconscious as a man of genius. I see him as he turns, Anglo-Saxon from skin to core; sixty and more by the almanack, but fifty by himself; vigorous and bluff, full of healthy power of body and of mind. I see him, true, straightforward, honest; staunch as a friend; hearty, but not vindictive, as a hater; generous in his blame as in his praise, glowing with enthusiasm for a young painter's success, or flushed with anger at a folly or a wrong. And then he smiles again – that smile of extraordinary sweetness and significance, which ever and anon lights up the handsome face, and strikes the key-note to all that is tender in his work, all that is graceful and loveable in his pictures of passion or of beauty, in woman, man, or child.

And then again I see him: little changed; the kindness of his manner what it ever was, the geniality of his friendship as gentle and cordial as before the cloud had gathered. But it is difficult to hear him now, and the strain of talking is great. He stops in the course of a sentence, and pointing in apology to his throat, he laughingly rounds off the conversational fragment with a knowing side-shake of the head. Once more I see him, forgetful of his dying self, striding off to the hospital to cheer a member of the Academy lying ill – for he is now the President, and father of his flock. Then, he vanishes from sight – to his room of sickness, agony, and death. And word comes out to us of his heroism, his gentleness, his patient suffering, whispered tales of the old white-bearded man, wasted, worn, and dumb, but bright and handsome still – who yet has a warm and lusty grip for the one or two who may say good-bye, and a faint smile of happy greeting that shows he is the old Millais still. And then —— We are spared the rest. And this is the end of a bright and sunny life – the cruel lining to a cloud of purple and of gold.

Illustrations

Images on pp. 14, 47, 80 and 85 courtesy V&A Museum, London
Other images ARC

First published 2007 by
Pallas Athene,
42 Spencer Rise,
London NW5 1AP

www.pallasathene.co.uk

© Pallas Athene 2007

ISBN 1 84368 034 3/978 1 84368 034 5

Printed in China

This book is part of our series Lives of the Artists,
*presenting biographies of artists by their contemporaries,
many of them published for the first time.
To find out more visit our website,
www.livesoftheartists.co.uk*

Note on the text:

Millais' *Thoughts on our art of today* was first published
in *The Magazine of Art* in 1888 (vol. 11, pp. 289-292).
It was reprinted by M. H. Speelmann in a slightly
edited version in the same volume
as the *Sketch* of Millais' life, in 1898.
To keep the flavour of Millais' prose and punctuation,
we have used the original edition of the *Thoughts*.